NEUROMARKETING
Is There a 'Buy Button' in the Brain?

How Selling to the OLD BRAIN will Bring You Instant Success

Patrick Renvoisé and Christophe Morin

ISBN #0-9743482-2-8

For information, please contact SalesBrain LLC at info@salesbrain.net

Cover Design by Jay Cabalquinto of Philippe Becker Design
www.pbdsf.com

© Custom Photos by Frederic Neema of Frederic Neema Photography
www.fnphoto.com

© Custom Illustrations by Xplane
www.xplane.com

Special thanks go to Bonnie Bright for her significant intellectual, design and editorial contribution. Thanks also go to Frederic Neema of Frederic Neema Photography, Dave Gray of XPlane, David Becker, Philippe Becker, and Jay Cabalquinto of Philippe Becker Design, Benson Lee of DSignWright, Rick Crandall, Gail DaMert, and the many people who helped make this book a reality.

To my wife, Nathalie for her unconditional support during the long and lonely months of research work that led to this book. Her love is a constant source of energy.

To our son Theo. At the age of 5, he already knows how to sell to our OLD BRAIN.

-- Patrick Renvoisé

To Bonnie for her support, love, and for giving me the strength to be true to myself and my passion.

To my sons Elliott and Oliver, hoping that they will use principles of this book to increase their future success and happiness.

-- Christophe Morin

NEUROMARKETING

Foreword by Patrick Renvoisé

Late in 2001, after spending most of my adult life in sales, I took advantage of a break in my career to research and develop a new understanding of Sales and Marketing. During nine months of retreat and extensive research in sales, marketing, and neuroscience--integrated with my years of experience in closing complex transactions--I developed the basis of a method called the *Selling to OLD BRAIN,* now recognized as the first proven *Neuromarketing* approach to closing Sales.

I shared my work with a longtime friend, Christophe Morin. Christophe and I always joked about our respective professional biases. He was a "marketing" guy, and I was a "sales" guy. When I asked him to review the first draft of my book, his diagnosis was the following: "I love the theory and I am amazed that you have found a way to merge the best of marketing thinking with the best of sales thinking."

That was the good news! "However," he continued in his usual manner, "I think the development of your key marketing concepts needs some fine-tuning." I wasn't surprised. Having huge respect for Christophe's highly successful career in marketing and management, I put him to the challenge. "Why don't you rewrite the sections you think should be improved and help me finish the book?"

By now, you know the end of the story. For twelve solid months, Christophe and I partnered to finesse the book and present a solid, proven formula to increase anyone's selling effectiveness. The book is still narrated by me, Patrick, as when I first produced the draft back in late 2001. You'll find it packed with stories, examples, and an effective, scientific formula for success. Enjoy!

Patrick Renvoisé

PS:

In 2002, Christophe and I founded SalesBrain, a company whose purpose is to lead the charge in Neuromarketing by applying the *Selling to the OLD BRAIN* method through Research, Consulting, and Training. Since SalesBrain was founded, we have trained hundreds of sales executives and have received exceptional ratings and a multitude of wonderful success stories about the measurable impact of our groundbreaking approach.

Neuromarketing has since emerged as a powerful and exciting new branch on the Marketing tree. SalesBrain continues to grow and has been nominated twice to receive the "Next Big Thing in Marketing" award by the AMA--American Marketing Association. Neuromarketing is critical to you as both a consumer and as a marketer, and we invite you to learn more about it.

TABLE OF CONTENTS

NEUROMARKETING

INTRODUCTION

Have you ever been in a sales situation where you were absolutely convinced you had the best solution for your prospect, but you still lost the deal? Even the best of us have experienced this paradox.

Selling today is tougher than ever because:
- Buyers are more sophisticated
- Competition is more intense
- Sales cycles are longer
- Buying by committee is more common
- Resistance to normal closing techniques has increased

Fortunately, learning about Neuromarketing will quickly increase your selling effectiveness, enabling you to "push your target's 'Buy Buttons'" and rapidly achieve the following:

- Deliver convincing sales presentations
- Shorten your sales cycle
- Close more deals
- Boost your revenue and profits
- Radically improve your ability to influence others

You will also learn how to craft compelling messages in your marketing material and on your web site that will bring you a constant flow of new prospects. These techniques can also be used to raise money for your business or to gain new jobs or promotions.

But, before we enter into the science of the OLD BRAIN, let me tell you a short story about my best customer ever. Even though he was homeless, I made $960 an hour consulting for him. Here is how it happened:

One evening, as I was entering a restaurant in San Francisco, a homeless person stopped me. He was displaying an all-too-common cardboard sign that said:

He showed all the signs of distress with a sad emptiness in his eyes; a poor fellow indeed. I do not pretend to be an altruist, but often, when some of these poor people look me directly in the eyes, my conscience demands that I hand over a dollar or two. But, on this occasion, I decided to go one step further than giving him a dollar: I

wanted to increase his selling effectiveness. You know what they say: "It's better to teach a man to fish than to give him a fish."

The first challenge my would-be client faced was the same that many individuals or companies face: his message was weak, and certainly not unique. There are thousands of homeless people in San Francisco and they are all asking for "help". So I handed over two dollars under one condition: that he would let me change the message on his cardboard sign for at least two hours. I even promised him an additional $5 if he was still there when I got out of the restaurant. I wanted to give him an incentive to try even if he thought my message wouldn't work.

I picked up his cardboard sign and on the reverse side, I wrote down a new message. He agreed to use it as I walked inside the restaurant with my friends. Two hours later, as we met him again on our way out, he refused to take my $5. Instead, the homeless man insisted on giving me $10! He happily explained to me he had made $60 in the two hours that I was eating dinner.

He normally averaged between $2 and $10 an hour so he was truly thankful. He forced me to accept his $10, and since the entire interaction had lasted only 30 seconds, this $8 profit translates into $960 an hour.

What did his new cardboard sign say?

I did not realize at the time why this message had unparalleled impact: it spoke a powerful language understood by the true decision-maker, a language that will change sales and marketing principles forever.

So why should you read this book?
Because it is the fastest way to go from this...

To this...

There are over 14,000 books covering sales and marketing. Throughout our careers, Christophe and I have read a great number of those books and attended every major sales and marketing training program on the market. However, at the end of each new book or program, we always felt that our selling effectiveness had increased by only a few points at best!

Current books and training programs focus primarily on the tactical issues relating to lead generation, prospect qualification, funnel management, and decision-maker identification.

This book is the *only one* that introduces you to a new language which, once learned, helps you build and deliver messages that influence the true decision-maker: the OLD BRAIN. Simple and easy-to-remember, the language of the OLD BRAIN offers a unique communication platform that dramatically increases your selling effectiveness, allowing you to reach a sustained higher level of success in all your sales, marketing, and communication efforts. An that's the promise of Neuromarketing!

NEUROMARKETING

CHAPTER 1

THREE BRAINS:
ONE DECISION-MAKER

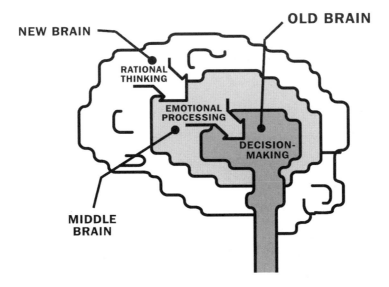

Having the best technology or the highest quality solution does not guarantee that prospects will always buy from you. Exciting new findings in brain research suggest that speaking to the true decision-maker, the OLD BRAIN, will raise your effectiveness in communicating an idea or selling a product.

You probably already know that a distinction is often made between the left brain and the right brain. The left hemisphere is the center of linear thinking such as language, logic, and mathematics. The right hemisphere is the center of conceptual thoughts such as art, music, creativity, and inspiration.

The brain is also categorized into three distinct parts which act as separate organs with different cellular structures and different functions. Although the three parts of the brain communicate with each other, each one has a specialized function:

- **The New Brain *thinks*.** It processes rational data and shares its deductions with the other two brains.

- **The Middle Brain *feels*.** It processes emotions and gut feelings and also shares its findings with the other two brains.

- **The OLD BRAIN *decides*.** It takes into account the input from the other two brains, but the OLD BRAIN is the actual trigger of decision.

The OLD BRAIN is a primitive organ. It is our "fight or flight" brain, our survival brain--and is also called the reptilian brain because it is still present in reptiles today. It exists as a direct result of the basic evolutionary process. According to leading neuroscientist, Robert Ornstein, in *The Evolution of Consciousness*, the OLD BRAIN is still concerned only with our survival as it has been for millions of years.

In fact, the body of research that demonstrates the prevalence of the OLD BRAIN in the decision-making process is overwhelming, and yet, it is ignored by traditional sales and marketing approaches.

In the book, *How the Brain Works*, human brain scientist, Leslie Hart, observes, "Much evidence now indicates that the OLD BRAIN is the main switch in determining what sensory input will go to the new brain, and what decisions will be accepted."

In his book *Descartes' Error*, Professor Antonio Damasio, Head of Neurology at Iowa Universit,y one of the foremost experts in the brain/decision-making processes states, "The lower levels in the neural edifice of reason are the same ones that regulate the processing of emotions and feelings along with the bodily functions necessary for an organism's survival...Emotion, feeling and biological regulation all play a role in human reason. The lowly orders of our organism are in the loop of higher reason."

Michael Tomasello, a cognitive scientist and Codirector of the Max Planck Institute for evolutionary Anthropology in Germany writes, "The 6 million years that separate human beings from other great apes is a very short time evolutionarily, with modern humans and chimpanzees sharing 99% of their genetic material...There simply has not been enough time for normal processes of biological evolution involving genetic variation and natural; selection to have created one by one each of the cognitive skills necessary for modern humans to invent and maintain complex tool-use industries and technologies, complex forms of symbolic communication."

Other works that highlight the role and importance of the OLD BRAIN include *You've Got to be Believed to be Heard* by Bert Decker, who develops the concept of achieving trust via the OLD BRAIN in order to generate understanding and *Emotional Intelligence* by Daniel Goleman who also reviews the working principals of the OLD BRAIN.

Finally, in *Emotional Brain*, Dr. Joseph LeDoux points out that the amygdala--a part of the OLD BRAIN--has a greater influence on the cortex than the cortex has on the amygdala, allowing emotional arousal to dominate and control thinking.

WHAT TO REMEMBER

Researchers have demonstrated that human beings make decisions in an emotional manner and then justify them rationally. Furthermore, we now know that the final decision is made by the OLD BRAIN.

CHAPTER 2

THE ONLY SIX STIMULI THAT SPEAK TO THE OLD BRAIN

So how do you systematically reach the true decision-maker, the OLD BRAIN? The OLD BRAIN, in addition to processing input directly from the New Brain and the Middle Brain, responds to six very specific stimuli, which, if mastered, give you the key to unlocking the language the OLD BRAIN understands.

1. The OLD BRAIN is *self-centered.* Think of the OLD BRAIN as the center of ME. It has no patience or empathy for anything that does not immediately concern its well-being and survival. If you had the misfortune of seeing someone injured right in front of your eyes, your OLD BRAIN wouldn't really care: it simply can't afford to. It's just relieved that *you're* not the one who got hurt. Emotionally, of course, you may empathize or, rationally, you may be concerned about the consequences of what just occurred, but this reaction occurs at the Middle or New brain level.

2. The OLD BRAIN is sensitive to solid *contrast* such as before/after, risky/safe, with/without, and slow/fast. *Contrast* allows the OLD BRAIN to make quick, risk-free decisions. Without *contrast*, the OLD BRAIN enters a state of confusion, which ultimately results in delaying a decision, or worse, making no decision at all.

3. The OLD BRAIN needs *tangible* input: it is constantly scanning for what is familiar and friendly; what can be recognized quickly, what is concrete and immutable. The OLD BRAIN cannot process concepts like "a flexible solution", "an integrated approach", or "a scalable architecture" without a lot of effort and skepticism. It appreciates simple, easy-to-grasp, concrete ideas like "more money", "unbreakable", and "24-hour turnaround time".

4. The OLD BRAIN remembers *the beginning and end* but forgets most everything in between. This short attention span has huge implications on how you should construct and deliver your messages. Placing the most important content at the beginning is a must, and repeating it at the end an imperative. Keep in mind that anything you say in the middle of your delivery will be mostly overlooked.

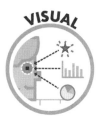

5. The OLD BRAIN is *visual*. Neuroscience demonstrates that when you see something that looks like a snake, your OLD BRAIN warns you instantly of danger so that you react even before the New Brain physically recognizes it's a snake. The optical nerve is physically connected to the OLD BRAIN and is 25 times faster than the auditory nerve. Therefore, the visual channel provides a fast and effective connection to the true decision-maker.

6. The OLD BRAIN is strongly triggered by *emotion*. Neuroscience has clearly demonstrated that emotional reactions create chemical events in your brain that directly impact the way you process and memorize information. In fact, you simply can't remember events and information for anything more than short-term unless you experience what some scientists refer to as a strong "emotional cocktail": the result of emotions being

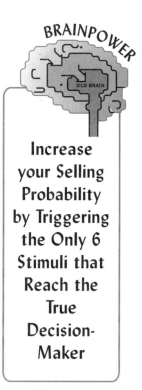

Increase your Selling Probability by Triggering the Only 6 Stimuli that Reach the True Decision-Maker

chemically processed by the brain.

WHAT TO REMEMBER

The OLD BRAIN responds to only 6 stimuli. Mastering these 6 stimuli immediately gives you the capacity to sell better, to be more efficient in marketing, and in all forms of communication.

CHAPTER 3

THE METHODOLOGY:
FOUR STEPS TO SUCCESS

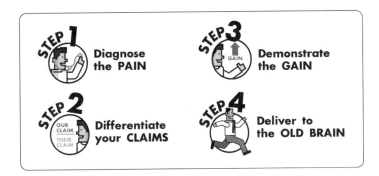

STEP 1 Diagnose the PAIN

STEP 2 Differentiate your CLAIMS

STEP 3 Demonstrate the GAIN

STEP 4 Deliver to the OLD BRAIN

"Creating a new theory is not like destroying an old barn and erecting a skyscraper in its place. It is rather like climbing a mountain, gaining new and wider views, and discovering unexpected connections between our starting point and its rich environment."

-- Albert Einstein, Physicist

To help you sell, market, or influence more effectively, this book translates the six stimuli into four easy action steps. To help your OLD BRAIN remember these four steps, we have made them rhyme.

The 4 Steps of Selling to the OLD BRAIN

You will directly increase your Selling Probability when you follow these four fundamental steps:

1. **Diagnose the PAIN** and craft a message that concretely demonstrates to your prospect how you will cure it

2. **Differentiate your CLAIMS** from those of your competitors

3. **Demonstrate the GAIN** that your solution provides to your prospect

4. **Deliver to the OLD BRAIN** in a way that has maximum impact

Diagnose the PAIN

Diagnose the PAIN

In this step you should ask the right questions and carefully listen to your prospects. The true PAIN often lies below the conscious level, so be prepared to unveil PAIN they did not even know they had.

Since the OLD BRAIN is *self-centered* and concerned with its

16

own survival above all else, it is highly interested in solutions that will alleviate any PAIN it is feeling.

If you're selling drills, your prospects really couldn't care less about the drills. What they actually want are the holes. Your diagnostic should consist of bringing to light all the issues they have about the holes they need to make...not the drills.

Combining your expert knowledge with their own understanding and interpretation of their current situation and their desired outcome will lead to an accurate Diagnostic of their PAIN.

 **Differentiate your CLAIMS**

Differentiate your CLAIMS

Have you noticed that approximately 95% of all web sites or brochures start with the same sentence: "We are one of the leading providers of..." This is an empty CLAIM that works against you. To reach the OLD BRAIN more effectively, this book will teach you new ways to say and to prove the statement, "We are the *only* provider of..."

As you have learned, the OLD BRAIN responds favorably to good, solid contrast. Powerful, unique CLAIMS attract prospects. They also simplify purchasing decisions.

Your prospects will always be thinking of two contrasting scenarios, whether they ever come up in your conversation or not:

- How does this compare to other options? and

- How does this compare to my doing nothing?

So ask yourself, "Is my solution uniquely able to cure my prospect's PAIN?"

If you can quickly point to what is absolutely different and valuable about your solution, then you create the contrast that the OLD BRAIN is looking for. More importantly, you become the only vendor that can solve their PAIN.

Demonstrate the GAIN

Demonstrate the GAIN

Listing and talking about the unique benefits of your solution as recommended in Step #2 is all well and good, but it doesn't technically prove anything. Remember, the OLD BRAIN prefers *tangible*. It needs solid proof about how your solution will enable it to survive or to benefit. Since the OLD BRAIN can't decide unless it feels secure, it is not enough to simply describe the value of your product or service; you need to concretely demonstrate the GAIN your prospects get from your solution--a specific cure to their number one PAIN--in a way that satisfies the OLD BRAIN's need for concrete evidence.

Remember, when it comes to communicating the benefits of your solution, it's not just about value. It's about proven value!

Deliver to the OLD BRAIN

Deliver to the OLD BRAIN

The latest brain research clearly demonstrates that the OLD BRAIN always makes the final call! When you deliver your message, your impact is directly linked to your ability to sell to the decision-making part of your prospect's brain by speaking to it directly, in a language it understands, through the six stimuli that trigger a response. In fact, your ability to deliver directly to the OLD BRAIN affects your selling probability as much as the three other factors--PAIN, CLAIMS, and GAIN--combined. That's why it has a cubic function in our formula:

$$\text{Your Selling Probability} = \text{Pain} \times \text{Claim} \times \text{Gain} \times (\textbf{OLD BRAIN})^3$$

Let's take a simple example: using all four steps in our formula, imagine you are selling water.

1) The more thirst--translate **PAIN**--your prospects are experiencing, the more potential you have to sell them water.

2) If you have two competitors who also sell water and assuming that your **CLAIMS** are equally strong as those of your two competitors--your selling probability is immediately divided by three.

3) Now, let's assume that your unique CLAIM is that your water is the most refreshing. The more strongly you are able to *prove* what your customer will **GAIN** by drinking your "most refreshing" water, the more chance you will have to close the sale.

4) Finally, imagine you and your two competitors are selling water in the middle of a desert. As a way to impact your prospects' OLD BRAINS, you could advertise your water using a large billboard with a fountain of actual cold water flowing out of it while giving away small samples for them to taste. This surely would have more impact than just using a static sign, no matter how large, that said: "Fresh Water".

Applying the Four Steps of *Selling to the OLD BRAIN* requires method and discipline, but the rewards are well worth the effort. The four upcoming chapters will cover each of the four steps in detail.

Since this book is the *only* neuromarketing book based on a remarkable, innovative combination of the latest brain research and cutting edge sales, marketing, and communication techniques, you can begin to use these techniques immediately to turn your newfound knowledge into action to develop and deliver messages that will change the way you influence forever.

WHAT TO REMEMBER

You will directly increase your chances to sell if you follow the 4 fundamental steps:

1. Diagnose the PAIN and construct a message that concretely shows your prospect how you can eliminate it.

2. Differentiate your CLAIMS from those of your competitors or other offerings in your field.

3. Demonstrate the GAIN that your solution offers to your prospect.

4. Deliver to the OLD BRAIN to get the most impact.

Important Note

All you need to remember about the Selling to the OLD BRAIN method is found a a large graphical poster inserted into this book. I recommend you post it near you in order to have an overview that will serve as a point of reference while you read. Remember that the OLD BRAIN is visual! If you follow visually where you are in the process as you progress, you will improve your comprehension and your memorization of the Selling to the Old Brain method. You will see that the first section of the poster summarizes effectively what we have already covered.

CHAPTER 4

STEP 1: DIAGNOSE THE PAIN
No PAIN, No GAME

"One of the best ways to persuade others is with your ears--by listening to them."

-- Dean Rusk, Former U.S. Secretary of State

Your Selling Probability = PAIN x Claim x Gain x (Old Brain)^3

How would you feel if you were sick and your doctor prescribed a remedy without listening to you describe your symptoms first? How much faith would you have in his remedy? Similarly, how do you feel when a salesperson tries to sell you a product without understanding your PAIN or sources of stress and tension first?

Before prescribing medication, a doctor questions his or her patient and typically initiates a dialogue that helps unveil the true source of the PAIN. From this information, the doctor formulates a diagnosis, which is shared with the patient. Often the doctor makes an effort to ensure that the patient really understands and accepts the diagnosis. By doing so, the doctor can be more confident that the patient will follow instructions and take the prescribed medication.

If you think about it, people who buy drills have a specific PAIN that really has nothing to do with drills: what they really want is what the holes can do for them, like hanging a picture or remodeling their kitchen.

By taking the time to carefully probe your prospect's PAIN, you achieve several goals:

- you help them unveil the true source of their PAIN

- you establish your expertise by the appropriateness or

relevance of your questions

- you establish valuable trust with their OLD BRAIN.

Years ago, a pizza company did a survey to uncover the number one PAIN of customers who ordered home-delivered pizza. What do you think it was? The taste of the pizza? How hot or cold it was? Getting it fast? Actually, the number one PAIN was measured as *not knowing when the pizza would arrive*. Armed with this vital information, Domino's Pizza established a very successful slogan: *Thirty minutes or less (or it's free)*. This is a strong example of how diagnosing the PAIN and showing your prospects how you can solve it will make your solution highly compelling.

Can you and every person you work with state the number one PAIN of your prospects? Are you absolutely certain you are selling benefits that are correctly aligned with their number one PAIN?

Let's look at what happened to Christophe Morin, co-author of this book, while heading the US subsidiary of a flag and sign manufacturing company.

How can you win a multi-million dollar, highly competitive American Olympic contract when you are a foreign-owned business with little US presence, and your solution is the most expensive one on the market?

The answer is by doing the best diagnostic of your prospect's PAIN:

I spent two and half years visiting ACOG (Atlanta Committee for the Olympic Game) from 1993 to 1996. It took this much time to understand ACOG's complex and ever-changing organizational chart and to discover what the dominant financial, strategic, and personal expectations of the buying committee responsible for flags, flagpoles, flag ceremonies, and flag logistics were.

My meticulous and tedious process led me to a surprising conclusion: ACOG's PAIN was mostly personal. Buyers were deeply worried about the embarrassing, if not devastating, impact of a diplomatic incident. You may never have thought about this, but raising or flying a flag can have multiple sensitive issues associated with it. For instance, what is the proper protocol for raising a flag in an indoor venue? How should it be handled and folded? Who will view the flag and how will it appear from each angle? How high does it need to go logistically so it can be seen properly? How do you make sure that the design of a particular country has been officially approved or updated?

These are exactly the PAIN factors I focused on. During the development of the RFQ (Request for Quote), I insisted that we had the highest level of competency in the art and science of flags (vexillology) and could claim to be the only company in the world that had developed an officially approved digital database of flag designs. With these unique CLAIMS clearly and comprehensively articulated --addressing an obvious and profound understanding of ACOG's PAIN --I was able to overcome the overwhelming odds against us and close a multi-million-dollar deal.

Now, let's look at the best way to diagnose the PAIN. The *Selling to the OLD BRAIN* theory defines PAIN as the difference between a desired state and an existing state. To properly diagnose a prospect's PAIN, you simply need to answer the following four questions:

1. *What is the source of the prospect's most prominent PAIN?*

2. *What level or degree is the intensity of that PAIN?*

3. *What is the level of urgency requiring the PAIN to be solved?*

4. Is my prospect aware of and does he/she acknowledge his/her own PAIN?

Source of the PAIN

PAIN always falls into three main categories: Financial PAIN, Strategic PAIN, and Personal PAIN.

Financial PAIN: this category covers the economic performance or lack thereof. Sales revenues, profitability, and ROI are good examples. Financial PAIN is typically highly visible and easy to measure.

Strategic PAIN: this category includes issues that affect the business processes used to develop, manufacture, and sell products or services. Typical strategic types of PAIN include poor product quality, declining market share, and higher business risk. Strategic PAIN is not as visible as financial PAIN and cannot always be easily measured.

Personal PAIN: this category is made up of the feelings and *emotions* affecting those who are involved in decision-making and the resolution of the PAIN. Good examples of personal PAIN is a high level of stress, job insecurity, or longer working days.

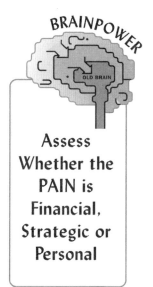

Assess Whether the PAIN is Financial, Strategic or Personal

Defining the source of the PAIN is like taking a patient's pulse at the right location. It is the best way to make sure your product or service is designed to bring effective relief. Take a look at this table (*See Figure 4.1*) to help you quickly define the source of your prospect's PAIN.

The first level of diagnosing the PAIN is best performed through extensive

	Areas of Pain & Tension	Methods of Measuring	Result/Fear Stimulated in the Old Brain
Financial	Lack of Funds Low Return on Investment	Data	Loss of Money
Strategic	Quality Issues Long Delivery Delays Long Product Development Cycles Lack of Strategy	Market Benchmarks Mappings Surveys Competitive Analysis	Loss of Business Control
Personal	Poor Attitude High Stress Lack of Motivation	Employee Surveys Leadership Assessments	Loss of Personal Energy

Figure 4.1 - Sourcing Your Prospect's PAIN

marketing research. Research can be conducted to:

1) explore PAIN

2) measure PAIN

In both instances, using surveys that ask the right questions is critical. All too often, the person or organization who designs the survey puts too much focus on descriptive variables such as demographics rather than *motivational* variables such as fears, desires, expectations, attitudes and satisfactions. This makes it nearly impossible to unveil the real PAIN.

To *explore* PAIN, you can conduct 12-16 in-depth interviews. Since your sample is so small, make sure you select very different prospects or customers depending on your focus. Stretching the boundaries of factors responsible for the PAIN is absolutely essential to produce a good qualitative assessment.

To *measure* PAIN, depending on total size of your market, you need bigger samples. For instance, for most Business to Consumer (B2C) markets, you will need at least 300 respondents to draw statistically meaningful results. At that sample size, there is a 95% confidence level that the actual population mean is within about 10% of the sample mean.

So, for example, on a yes-or-no question, if your mean is 20% for yes, you can be 95% confident that the actual mean would be between a minimum of 10% and a maximum of 30% if you were to survey the entire population.

Use the telephone, the web, face-to-face interview methods, or a combination of all three for best results. Note, however, that for these statistics to apply, the sample has to be random, or nearly so. Therefore, it is *not* desirable to include only volunteer respondents.

Intensity of the PAIN

The intensity of the PAIN is a crucial factor. You don't want to waste your time offering a cure for what may be a temporary itch. As you diagnose your prospect's PAIN, learn to measure its intensity. Low intensity is typically related to a low involvement or low urgency in the buying decision process. What this means is that the prospect or the organization will not commit major resources such as time, people, or money to the resolution of the PAIN and they may be harder to convince that they need a "cure" or a solution.

Learn to Detect and Focus on the High Intensity PAIN

High intensity PAIN manifests itself when large amounts of resources or efforts are drawn by the PAIN. Learn to diagnose whether the PAIN you are work-

BRAINPOWER

OLD BRAIN

Focus on the Most Time Sensitive PAIN Areas

ing to eliminate is of high or low intensity early in your selling process. Then focus on the high intensity PAIN!

Identifying the Urgency to Alleviate the PAIN

Knowing the *source* of the PAIN helps qualify the amount of tension or stress that is driving the intent to buy. Once you identify the source and intensity, you will know whether or not your prospect has powerful and compelling reasons to seek an imminent cure for the PAIN.

Urgency is a direct function of the consequences that will be felt if the PAIN is not cured. If the consequences are imminent or growing proportionately, then your prospect is more likely to act sooner than later. If there is not enough urgency, your prospect's OLD BRAIN will postpone a decision in order to deal with other priorities related to survival.

Acknowledgement of the PAIN

It is a critical part of the selling process to make sure your prospect acknowledges his or her own PAIN. Many times the common PAIN for which everyone is selling solutions has lots of competition. When you uncover a PAIN that is more unique or previously unrecognized, the prospect needs time to acknowledge it. Think about the last time you went to see a doctor. Most likely, after answering questions related to your ailment, you were asked to confirm that the diagnostic was realistic and reasonable.

In conclusion, the highest PAIN Factor is going to be found in the following case scenario (*See Figure 4.2*).

PAIN FACTOR

SOURCE	INTENSITY	TIMING	AWARENESS
Mainly Financial	High	Immediate	High
Loss of Money	Prospect is allocating multiple resources to eliminate the PAIN	Prospect's life or business will endure instant deterioration if no action is taken	Prospect is highly conscious and actively seeking a solution

Figure 4.2 - PAIN Factor

Many sales and marketing teams make the mistake of just promoting specific features of their product or service. Others, who are more experienced, transform those features into benefits. But, experts in *Selling to the OLD BRAIN* creatively diagnose their prospect's PAIN. Then, they address this PAIN with a solution that is customized and unique.

Let's examine this point: Sony once created an ad for video projectors which focused on one very specific PAIN they had identified. An ad like this *(See Figure 4.3)* which features the world of the prospects enhances the PAIN or trauma they feel. Notice how emphasizing a prospect's PAIN can have much higher impact on the OLD BRAIN than simply featuring the benefits of the projector or even picturing the projector itself. This works because the prospect's OLD BRAIN can relate to the self-centered, *visual* PAIN that is reenacted in the ad.

Also note the power of focusing on one

BRAINPOWER

Ensure that your Prospect Acknowledges his or her PAIN

Figure 4.3 - Focus on the PAIN

main benefit of a projector: its small size and light weight. Notice how an actual projector isn't even visible in the picture. By re-enacting the PAIN--*not* by emphasizing the features of their projector--this ad speaks to the OLD BRAIN.

Asking Open Questions

In the diagnostic phase of the sales process, you should always start by asking open-ended questions, questions that cannot be answered with 'yes' or 'no'. These questions will invite your prospects to reflect on their PAIN and eventually come to acknowledge its severity and/or urgency.

At this early stage, you should drive the diagnostic without real attachment to winning the business: if your prospect's PAIN cannot be cured by your product or service, then you should move on and look for another prospect. The soft-selling approach adds great credibility for you and builds trust for the future. However, if your product or service can solve the top PAIN of the prospect, then positioning the unique benefits of your products, i.e. your CLAIMS, early in the sales cycle will inevitably disqualify your competitors.

Start your Sales Process with Open Questions

Manuel Hoffmann is a Director of Marketing at a high tech company in Silicon Valley. His favorite tool to help jumpstart the dialogue with his prospects is to invite them to use a white board.

"In my first meetings with them," Manuel says, "I really want to understand their PAIN. As I listen to their issues and challenges, I often draw a picture on the white board. Then I ask them if this is correct and I hand them the pen. It's amazing what people are willing to reveal if you are willing to listen and truly understand

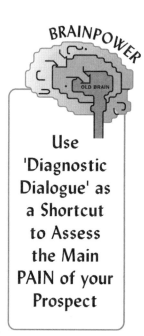

Use 'Diagnostic Dialogue' as a Shortcut to Assess the Main PAIN of your Prospect

their PAIN points."

Diagnostic Dialogue

If your process allows for an individual interview with your prospect, you should adopt a "Diagnostic Dialogue" technique.

In his renowned book, *On Dialogue*, world-famous Quantum Physicist, Dr. David Bohm, offers four fundamental rules to conducting an effective dialogue. In order to explore your prospect's PAIN and lead to an accurate assessment of his or her PAIN, you should use these four principles because they ensure the optimum flow of ideas and thoughts which ultimately lead to quick understanding:

Principles of Effective Dialogue
1-Suspend your judgment

By holding back your opinions, you release the tight grip on your preconceived positions. You create a climate of trust and intimacy in which your prospect feels free to open up and take a good introspective look at his/her situation.

2-Listen carefully

The way you listen directly impacts your capacity to learn and build quality PAIN diagnostics. True listening means that you allow others' ideas and opinions to influence yours. Your attention and your body movement must convey this state to your prospect. Listening also involves actively searching for the meaning behind the words instead of impatiently waiting for the other person to stop speaking so you can jump in with your own thoughts.

3-Challenge assumptions

Assumptions are like dirty glasses. We look through them and we sometimes draw wrong conclusions about what we see. Our perception may actually be distorted based on our own experience. It is always better to state your perception-with awareness that it is *your* perception and make sure the other person in the dialogue sees it the same way. Revisiting assumptions enables you to build your dialogue from a platform of truth and clarity.

4-Inquire and reflect

Inquiry brings new information. Reflection brings new meaning to the information and creates a new perception of the relation-ships between various pieces of information. If you reflect on what your prospect says by accurately stating your prospect's points back to him, you can both assure that you understand his PAIN and probe deeper to generate further details. This fosters an environment for creative thinking that builds on past experiences versus reliving the same pattern over and over again. In short, it creates new ideas.

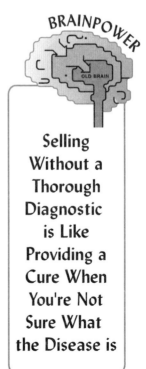

Sales and Marketing professionals strong in *Selling to the OLD BRAIN* apply these rules naturally. They create a climate in which the prospect also adopts and follows these rules for a deeper dialogue. The deeper the dialogue, the more chances you have to discover the real PAIN.

Take heed: a common mistake often made is to start selling too early. Selling too early without a diagnostic is like trying to provide a cure when you are not sure what the disease is. If you jump into a description of features and benefits without taking the time to assess the

NEUROMARKETING

PAIN, your prospect may believe that you are specialized in one particular area or offer something that is peripheral to what they really
need and to the PAIN they feel most urgently.

Probe Deeper with a PAIN Diagnostic

Your next challenge is to visit some of your prospects and customers and conduct a thorough PAIN Diagnostic. Use the four
"Rules of Dialogue": (1) withhold opinions, (2) listen carefully, (3)
challenge assumptions, and (4) reflect.

For more measurable and *tangible* results, you should conduct
a formal marketing survey that will help you unveil the true PAIN
by asking deeper motivational questions. It is critical that your
prospects' PAIN is brought to their awareness.

Use caution in your diagnostic process: if you sell the same
products to different groups or types of people, your prospects'
PAIN might be significantly different from one group to another. To
address clusters of prospects, it is more effective to confirm and
verify the common PAIN of each cluster. If you are selling to individual prospects, it is even better to confirm the PAIN for each
individual prospect. If you are selling to a group, you may need to
confirm the personal PAIN of each one of the decision-influencers.

In *How Customers Think,* Gerald Zaltman, Professor at Harvard
Business school states, " Marketers need methods that go beyond
what customer can readily articulate –that get at what people don't
know they know...the more important is the unconscious mind."
And that is why careful Diagnostic of the PAIN is so important.

WHAT TO REMEMBER

A frequent error is attempting to sell too soon. Not having a thorough diagnostic is like trying to prescribe medication for someone when you don't know what their symptoms are. If you begin to describe the features and functions of your solution without taking the time to evaluate the PAIN of your prospect, he may end up believing your solution is too specific. Your solution must address his deepest PAIN.

CHAPTER 5

STEP 2: DIFFERENTIATE YOUR CLAIMS

No Claim, No Fame

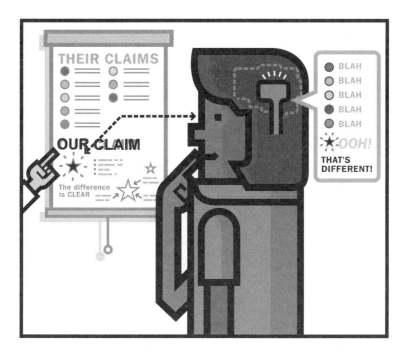

"In order to be irreplaceable one must always be different."

-- Coco Chanel, Fashion Designer

$$\text{Your Selling Probability} = \text{Pain} \times \textbf{CLAIM} \times \text{Gain} \times (\text{Old Brain})^3$$

If you are not selling something unique, you are selling as much for your competitors as you are selling for yourself.

If you have no competitors, or if your products or services are truly unique in the world, you can skip this chapter. If you read on, it is vital to define what is unique about your product or service before you can get the attention of the OLD BRAIN.

As you'll recall, *contrast* is one of the six stimuli that impacts the OLD BRAIN. CLAIMS create the evidence of a sharp *contrast* between your solution and all others offered by your competition.

Always Sell Something that is Perceived to be Totally Unique

The majority of corporate web sites start with the same sentence, "We are one of the leading providers of..." This CLAIM fails entirely to impact the OLD BRAIN. Why? It offers no contrast. The highest impact on the OLD BRAIN is achieved when you say, "We are the *only* provider of..."

Take bread, for example. Could there be a more general product? Is there a more competitive business than selling

38

bread in Paris? Isn't bread in Paris the ultimate commodity product?

For years, my own father has driven two miles every day to go to the same bakery. In his opinion, that particular bakery has the best bread in the area. The quality of their bread is known to be highly unique and my dad is so fanatic about bread that he is willing to drive the extra distance.

In contrast, when I lived in Paris, 99% of the time, I bought my bread from the bakery downstairs from my apartment. Although the bread at the downstairs bakery was only average, my main buying criteria was the fact that I didn't have to make any detour to buy my daily baguette: it was literally on the same sidewalk as my parking exit. I often came back late from work, and after a long stressful day, the idea of saving a few minutes of time was enough to keep me as a faithful customer. This bakery was the only bakery between the garage exit and the elevator that led to my apartment. That provided me with a unique benefit.

So every time you walk into a bakery or a coffee shop, ask yourself, "What is unique about this place that makes me buy here?" You'll quickly notice there is *always* something unique that explains your buying decision.

So how do you define your unique CLAIMS? Treat your solution as an invention and build your message firmly on your CLAIMS.

When inventors wish to register an invention, they must go through an

BRAINPOWER

CLAIM that You are "The ONLY One" Who Does or Has Something Specific

BRAINPOWER

Treat your Solution as an Invention and Build your Message Firmly on your CLAIMS

extensive patent registration process that culminates in the description of what are called "CLAIMS". In this process, an inventor must argue what features or benefits of his solution are completely new that no other invention has ever offered. In other words, it is part of the process that any features claimed as new be *contrasted* with what already exists.

Let's look at video projectors again to see how leading companies choose their CLAIMS and highlight them.

Main CLAIM: Our Projector is the *Smallest and Lightest*

Remember the earlier ad that focused on the prospect's PAIN of carrying heavy, large projectors? Here is an example of another ad *(See Figure 5.1)* that focuses on the same CLAIM--having the smallest and lightest projector--but uses a different approach.

Main CLAIM: Our Projector is the *Brightest*

In this ad, the CLAIM is all about the brightness of the image the projector displays *(See Figure 5.2)*. The PAIN being addressed is how poorly an image from another brand of projector shows up in brightly-lit rooms.

To differentiate yourself from the competition, choose one main CLAIM that correlates with your prospect's PAIN and address it in a powerful way. You can't miss the evident CLAIM in this ad of being the "brightest" projector on the market.

With our projector, size DOES matter

The 3999 series ProjectX projector is the smallest on the market. When you need to present, it fits right in a briefcase with room to spare. Don't get bogged down by dragging a dinosaur everywhere you go.

Figure 5.1 - Main CLAIM: Smallest Projector

If he
thinks
it's
bright
in here
now...

Wait 'til he sees our
projector

www.opuject.com

Figure 5.2 - Main CLAIM: Brightest Projector

Main CLAIM: Our Projector is the *Easiest to Use*

A third PAIN uncovered in the world of projectors is that of setting them up and using them. In this third example, a real ad from InFocus, the CLAIM is "extreme ease of use" *(See Figure 5.3)*.

In the three potential examples of CLAIMS we just reviewed, notice how each manufacturer differentiates its CLAIMS. They aren't selling "just another video projector". Instead, they sell:

- The *lightest* projector or
- The *brightest* projector or
- The *easiest* projector to use

By focusing on a specific CLAIM, each company emphasizes its own strength and tries to disqualify the competition.

What is unique about your solution?

If you have difficulties finding something unique about your business, look beyond pure technology or service differences. Be creative when you make your CLAIMS, like:

- the "original" such as Coke or Levi's
- "Number One" in sales (at the time): Hertz Rental Car
- the "recommended choice" as in "recommended by more doctors"
- "genuine" as in Russian Vodka or German cars

Avis' Unique Claim

How can a rental car company establish unique CLAIMS if they are not number one in sales? Traditionally, every rental car company rents out the same cars from the same airport counters and their services and pricing are almost identical.

Avis creatively found something unique about being Number Two to then-leader, Hertz. The slogan Avis adopted, "We Try Harder", implies that you will receive better service from them than from any of their competitors.

"We Try Harder" landed Avis the distinction of having the most recognized brand slogan in the rental car industry. Launched in 1963, "We Try Harder" has become synonymous with Avis, superior customer service, and going the extra mile.

The ubiquitous "We Try Harder" button is worn not only by Avis employees, but is often adopted by charitable volunteers to highlight their spirit and was even embraced, in camouflage version, by U.S. soldiers fighting in Vietnam.

WHAT TO REMEMBER

You need to find one or several unique attributes about your solution to strongly assert your CLAIMS. In choosing CLAIMS which eliminate the strongest principle PAIN of your prospects, you will strongly motivate them to buy from you. Your next task, then, is to demonstrate that they will get a substantial GAIN when they choose your product or your service.

CHAPTER 6

STEP 3: DEMONSTRATE THE GAIN
No Evidence, No Confidence

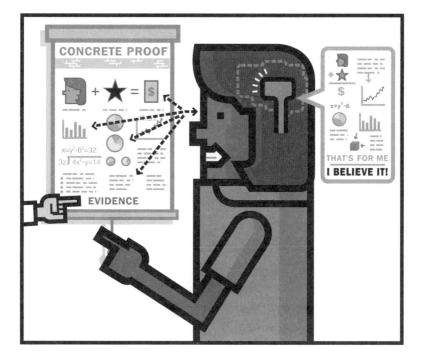

"Tell a man there are 300 billion stars in the universe and he'll believe you. Tell him the plate you're handing him is very hot and he'll have to touch it to believe you."

-- Mike Jaeger, Musician

> ## Your Selling Probability =
> ## Pain x Claim x GAIN x (Old Brain)3

By now, you have properly diagnosed the PAIN of your prospects and you have also discovered what unique CLAIMS you can make to position your offering as the best cure.

There are over 1,200 books that talk about the Value Proposition. The general advice they give is to show the highest possible value for your solution. Unfortunately, they all omit the importance of reaching the OLD BRAIN. Simply talking about the value is not enough: you have to *prove* it.

Because it controls our most primitive survival mechanisms, the true decision-maker, the OLD BRAIN, is especially resistant to adopting new ideas or behaviors. Some research has even suggested that the PAIN of making a change may be as harsh as physical torture. Be *tangible* and provide hard evidence if you want to increase your influence.

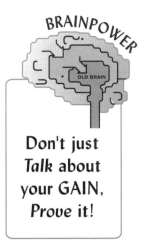

Don't just
Talk about
your GAIN,
Prove it!

You may think that because your product or service is a great value, it should sell itself. If the benefits of your solution are greater than its cost (the GAIN), your prospects would be foolish not to buy it from you. However, you need to deliver proof in terms the OLD BRAIN accepts.

A few years ago I was hired to help a start-up company raise money. Their product was a new device for portable phones or palm-tops, which they believed had the potential to become the de facto standard for all wireless devices of the future.

We had a first meeting set up with two people from a venture capital firm, John and Ron, the VCs, were using a large suite in a hotel by the airport where they had filled their entire agenda for the day with presentations from seven different start-ups. At 4:00 pm, our allotted timeslot, we knocked on their door.

They greeted us professionally, but with a definite lack of enthusiasm. We were the last to present that day and when Ron joked about the fact that we were the "last obstacle before their shower, a hot meal, and what would be a well-deserved night of sleep," I knew we had our work cut out for us.

As we set up for our presentation, John shared a bit of what their day had been like. He commented, "All six products we've seen today have great value propositions. All six founders are experienced and very enthusiastic, and all six of them have a perfectly laid out plan of how they will go public in six to twelve months."

However, John also volunteered the information that they were not particularly excited about making an investment in any of the companies they had seen because, in his words, "They've told us that their product is great and that there is a huge market for it. They've shown us the numbers they project, but they haven't actually proven anything."

Considering this new information and the seriousness of the sit-

uation, my client and I decided to skip our introduction and start directly with a proof of our value--an actual demo of our product.

We had a small prototype that perfectly illustrated what the product could do. In fact, it was so simple to use that the demo did not require any training and could be used by anybody, instantly.

I handed the device to John. It took about five seconds before he exclaimed enthusiastically, "This is cool! I get it!"

John and Ron spent the next 45 minutes playing with the different demos in the prototype. My client and I were beginning to think we were going to run out of time before we had a chance to tell them about the technology and the market.

It was 6:45 pm when we left their room that day with a commitment from them that they would send a team of their experts to review the technology and the nature of the investment. The prototype demo was an instant proof of value for John and Ron. Instead of just claiming value, we actually proved the value of our CLAIMS.

A couple of months later my client raised the money he was looking for.

So do you just *tell* people about your Value or do you *prove* them the GAIN?

The Value Must Outweigh the Costs

When a prospect decides to make a purchase, there is always a cost involved--whether it be Financial, Strategic, or Personal. Therefore, it is vital that you demonstrate the GAIN in a manner that is indisputable. GAIN is defined as the difference between the value of your solution minus its cost. If your prospect's OLD BRAIN does not perceive a relevant and *tangible* GAIN from your solution, it will never make the decision to buy.

Just like PAIN, GAIN can be broken down into three categories: Financial, Strategic, and Personal.

1. **The Financial GAIN** or ROI--Return On Investment--is proven when prospects see the evidence of measurable positive return on their purchase like saving money or increasing revenue or boosting profits.

2. **The Strategic GAIN** includes benefits that are less mea surable yet provide strategic enhancements to your business such as increased quality, faster product diversification, shorter market cycles, easier access to new markets. The Strategic GAIN cannot always be translated into financial GAIN.

3. **The Personal GAIN** relates to greater peace of mind, more fun, higher pride of ownership, improved chances for a promotion, a greater sense of accomplishment, more self-satisfaction, etc..

In a recent ad, IBM used this concept (*See Figure 6.1*) to illustrate the stress points an executive might personally experience in his life. Viewers can immediately relate to the multitude of thoughts and worries in progression around him.

Four Ways to Prove the GAIN

There are four ways to effectively demonstrate the GAIN to the OLD BRAIN. They are listed below from *most* effective to *least* effective. The effectiveness of each method is largely a function of how *tangible* and provable each one is.

1. A Customer Story: *80-100% Proof*
Imagine you are trying to sell your fabulous product to Ford and you have the benefit of already having sold a similar

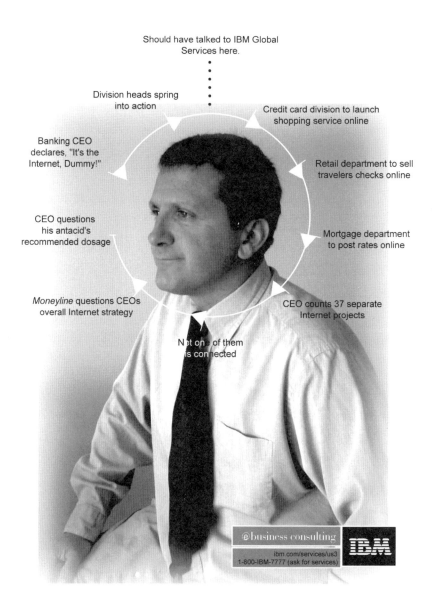

Figure 6.1 - Demonstrating the Personal GAIN

system to Chrysler. If you do a good job of illustrating the GAIN to Chrysler in a *tangible* way, how easy do you think it will be for Ford to draw a parallel between the benefits Chrysler is deriving from your system and what your prospects at Ford could get as well?

Customer stories are the strongest possible Proof of GAIN. The customer story you select should have a number of attributes in common with the prospect you are selling to. For example, you could say, "ABC company has been using our system for over three months now. They have saved an average of 5 cents per transaction." Since your prospect manufactures similar products and does 10,000 transactions per day, they can infer that they would potentially save $500 per day or $175,000 per year.

Of course, if the story comes directly from the customer in the form of a testimonial, it is even more powerful than if you require the customer to take your word for it. Hearing of your success from a peer in the following format will have even more impact: "We have been able to save 5 cents per transaction since we installed this new system." -- John Smith, VP Operations, ABC Company.

2. A Demo: *60-100% Proof*

A Demo is a short demonstration or proto-type of your product or service that proves the GAIN without necessarily going through all the features and functionality. Instead, it demon-strates one particular benefit or uniqueness. For example, you could show that your prospect could save 10 seconds per transaction, potentially creating a 5-cent savings per transaction.

Your Demos must be perfectly scripted and rehearsed to make sure they don't fail. Sometimes a simple picture or a written document from a credible source can constitute a strong Proof of GAIN. Depending on the nature of your CLAIMS and the relevance of your Demo to their PAIN, the Proof of GAIN of a Demo can be high.

3. Data: *20-60% Proof*

Let's take the following financial calculation as a Demonstration of GAIN, "Our product will save you an average of 5 cents per transaction and since you average 10,000 transactions a day, you will save $500 a day--or $175,000 per year." This calculation is based on two assumptions:

1) Your prospect is making 10,000 transactions per day. If this number has been provided by your prospect, then he/she will find it credible and *tangible.*

2) Your solution can truly save them 5 cents per transaction. This assumption may be harder to justify without testimonials or a solid demo, but it helps put a dollar sign to the Value.

You run a higher risk of your prospect's OLD BRAIN raising questions and concerns when presented with data than with customers' stories or demos. Data means numbers, which ultimately do not have as much impact on the OLD BRAIN. It's OK to use data if you don't have other options, but data works best if you can use it to *contrast* a situation like before and after.

Now, let's examine the least *tangible* demonstration of GAIN: a Vision.

4. A Vision: *10-40% Proof*

Imagine you are targeting a large car manufacturer with a new device that makes the use of a gearbox or an automatic transmission totally obsolete. If you don't have a sale or a customer testimonial yet, you may choose to use a "Vision" to Demonstrate the GAIN. For example, you could say, "Remember when the first CD players became available people did not really appreciate their benefits. Now, 20 years later, very few people still use turntables or cassettes. This is what our new transmission will do: it will render obsolete all previous technologies that transfer the energy from the engine to the wheels."

Steve Jobs, founder of Apple Computers was able to sell a vision of user-friendly, "cool" computers well before the technology could be demonstrated. If you choose a Vision, it will be more effective if you tell a story, use a metaphor, or create an analogy, as in the example above.

When you do not have any other way to Demonstrate the GAIN, a Vision can still help your prospect believe that they will receive benefits from your solution. This type of proof is much less effective than any of the previous techniques we discussed since it requires an act of faith from your prospect.

Organize your Proofs of GAIN

Organizing your Proofs of GAIN in the form of a matrix (*See Figure 6.2*) will help your prospects determine if they can derive most of the GAIN from the Financial, Strategic, or Personal area. It will also help you see if you are asking your prospects for an act of faith or if you are providing them with *tangible* Proofs.

For each GAIN statement, you should use at least one Proof of GAIN. To strengthen that proof--and if you believe it is a critical point--you can use more than one piece of evidence.

For example, if your prospect's PAIN is primarily financial, they will be highly interested in whether or not your solution can truly help them save money. You'll achieve much greater impact by using a powerful corresponding customer testimonial from a customer who experienced a significant financial GAIN along with providing your prospect with a Demo.

You have two effective options when presenting the Proof of GAIN to prospects: you can follow the matrix vertically by telling a story that includes all three categories--Financial, Strategic, and Personal--or you can use the matrix horizontally by giving several

Proof of GAIN Matrix for Your CLAIMS				
Proof / Gain	Customer Story	Demo	Data	Vision
Financial				
Strategic				
Personal				

Figure 6.2 - Proof of GAIN Matrix

proofs in any one of the four categories.

One element of the matrix can be a simple sentence like, "John Smith, VP of Manufacturing at ABC, saved $125,000 last year while using our new machine", or it can be a longer and more complex demonstration of the GAIN. However, by keeping it simple, you will help your prospect's OLD BRAIN accept the value statement.

Remember, the Proofs of GAIN are the core of your message. As supporting evidence of your CLAIMS, they must be *tangible*, factual, and provable in order to impact your prospect's OLD BRAIN. Make sure that every piece of information you share with your prospect has value for them. Ask yourself, "Am I training them on features and benefits or am I actually selling something that will appeal to their OLD BRAIN? Do I need to include this information to help them reach a decision or am I just diluting my value?" S*ell*, don't just "tell".

Main CLAIM: Our projector is small and lightweight

Remember seeing an ad earlier that features a projector between books (*see Figure 5.1*). What kind of GAIN does an ad which focuses on the size of the projector allude to: Financial, Strategic or Personal?

The answer is Personal GAIN: it suggests that by choosing a product from that particular manufacturer, you won't have to personally, physically drag a

Make the GAIN the Center of your Message

heavy, bulky projector with you whenever you're on the road. Therefore, the ad in *Figure 5.1* uses a Demo as proof of value: it *demonstrates* the value of a small size projector.

Again, part of the power of that ad was that it focused primar-

Proof of GAIN Matrix for Your CLAIMS				
Proof \ Gain	Customer Story	Demo	Data	Vision
Financial				
Strategic				
Personal		☑		

Figure 6.3 - Identifying Where your Proof of GAIN Applies

55

ily on the personal PAIN: all the other features of the projector were deliberately omitted and the Proof of GAIN was entirely based on one CLAIM: the small size of the projector.

Summary

Sales books often present arguments or tricks to create urgency in your prospects' minds to push them to make faster buying decisions. If you create a strong Proof of GAIN, you will never have to worry about creating that urgency: it will already be built right into your message. Why would your prospects delay the decision to buy if you have proven beyond reasonable doubt everything they will GAIN when they buy your solution?

If your prospects were rational thinking machines, sales and marketing strategies would only include these first three steps of *Selling to the OLD BRAIN*: Diagnosing the PAIN, Differentiating your CLAIMS, and Demonstrating the GAIN. However, human beings are not fully rational. All final decisions are made by our OLD BRAINS. Therefore, it is critical that you deliver your message in a manner that will directly impact the true decision-maker.

The next chapter explains how you can deliver the critical building blocks of your message in a way that easily maximizes your ability to influence the OLD BRAIN of your prospects.

WHAT TO REMEMBER

Most books dedicated to sales show you how to create urgency in the mind of your prospects in order to push them to make a quick purchase decision. But if you establish effective proof of your GAIN, you will never need to worry about creating this urgency: it will be inherently included in your message. Why would your prospect delay making a decision to buy if you have proven without rational doubt, visually and concretely, everything that they will GAIN by choosing your solution?

CHAPTER 7

STEP 4: DELIVER TO THE OLD BRAIN
No Connection, No Decision

"Power is not revealed by striking hard or often, but by striking true."

-- Honore De Balzac, French Author

> # Your Selling Probability =
> # Pain x Claim x Gain x $(\textbf{OLD BRAIN})^3$

Being unique by Differentiating your CLAIMS and proving your value by Demonstrating the GAIN are vital steps in impacting your audience. But alone, they are not enough. The most solid and logical message, though it may be of interest to your prospect, will still not trigger a buying decision unless the OLD BRAIN understands. Delivering your message with maximum impact to influence the real decision-maker, the OLD BRAIN, truly gives you the edge.

Building and Delivering Your Message for Ultimate Impact

For every message you create, you'll need to make use of a few special tools to have ultimate impact. Your *Selling to the OLD BRAIN* toolbox includes six Message Building Blocks and seven Impact Boosters that will gain you immediate attention and credibility with the OLD BRAIN.

Just as cells are the building blocks on which human life is based, each *Selling to the OLD BRAIN* Message Building Block is critical to the ultimate construction of a powerful message, and every Impact Booster will enhance these Building Blocks for maximum impact.

The more *Selling to the OLD BRAIN* tools you use when you build and deliver your message, the more immediate impact you will have on your audience's OLD BRAINS--ultimately helping you close deals and dramatically increasing your Selling Probability!

The Six *Selling to the OLD BRAIN* Message Building Blocks

1. Grabber
2. Big Picture
3. CLAIMS
4. Proofs of GAIN
5. Handling Objections
6. Close

Message Building Block #1: Grabbers

"If you grab attention in the first frame with a visual surprise, you stand a better chance of holding the viewer."

-- David Ogilvy, Advertising Expert

For survival reasons, it is in the best interest of your OLD BRAIN to be most alert at the beginning and at the end of interactions when change or an unknown new factor could cause danger. This is why *beginning and end* is one of the six stimuli to the OLD BRAIN which tends to pay less attention once security and familiarity is established in a given situation. When the OLD BRAIN becomes comfortable, it benefits more by going into an 'energy saving' mode and pays less attention to its surroundings.

Make a powerful impression early. Because *beginning and end* is so important to the OLD BRAIN, you need to grab your

Make a Strong First Impression by Creating a Powerful Grabber

prospects' attention early in your interaction or you may lose them forever. This applies to any form of communication you use including phone calls, faxes, emails, web sites, cold calls, and face-to-face presentations.

Keep the OLD BRAIN alert and attentive. Recall the last time you attended a seminar or convention. At the beginning of each presentation, your OLD BRAIN was wide-awake and on guard, scanning for the new and unfamiliar. In this mode, you achieved between 70% and 100% of maximum attention and retention.

As the presentation continued and your OLD BRAIN perceived that nothing seemed to be threatening its survival, it dropped its guard and went into "idle mode". At that point, your attention and retention dropped to 20% of the maximum level (*See Figure 7.1*) as suggested by George Morrisey and Thomas Sechrest in their book, *Loud and Clear: How to Prepare and Deliver Effective Business and Technical Presentations.*

Now, think about the last time you gave a presentation. Did you start with:

1. Who you are or what your background is?
2. The agenda of your presentation?
3. An overview of your company?
4. Features of your product or service?

If so, you probably wasted valuable time delivering details of little importance during the timeframe your prospect's OLD BRAIN was wide awake and chances are, you didn't get to the core of your message until your audience's OLD BRAINS started going into "idle

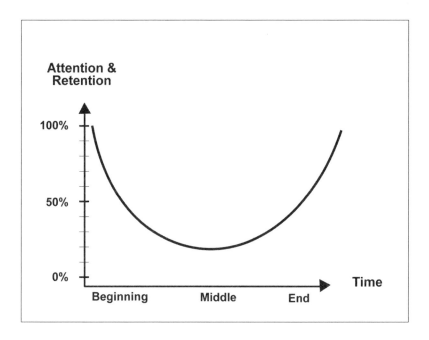

Figure 7.1 - Measuring Attention & Retention

mode". What a missed opportunity to deliver the highlights of your story to the true decision-maker!

Don't waste valuable information by delivering it at an inopportune time. Typically, many individuals present the most important content too late in their presentations. Take a product demo as an example: your demo might contain two or three golden "nuggets" that could really change your prospect's life with unique, measurable GAIN. But if you catch your prospect at a low attention level, he or she will miss the GAIN entirely. You just lost a valuable opportunity that you can never recapture! Most demos are just a long list of features with no real connection to a *tangible* GAIN or a solution for the PAIN.

The purpose of using a Grabber is to present your GAIN upfront. Just like mining for gold, your prospects will stay attentive longer if they actually discover several nuggets in the first three minutes.

Make a strong first impression. Grabbers have tremendous impact because you only have one chance to make a first impression. The OLD BRAIN is quick to judge and label so it can immediately categorize and recognize a potential threat. Once judgement is passed, it's very difficult for the OLD BRAIN to change its first impression. Begin your presentation or message with a Grabber that is centered around your prospect's most prominent PAIN and you'll set the stage for a great start.

You can develop a higher understanding of this process by examining the natural 'human resistance curve'. (*See Figure 7.2*) This curve shows the natural human response to any new idea or message. The solid line represents an average adoption curve that does not have a Grabber. The dotted line shows how one adopts the concept more easily and more quickly when one is exposed to a message where a strong Grabber is used.

By using a Grabber, you ensure that your prospects will go through the five phases of Human Resistance Curve much faster. Moreover, their overall reactions will remain more positive in the long run.

Print ads are frequently just big Grabbers: there isn't the time or space to present anything else, so the message has to catch the reader's attention right away. Humor is another type of Grabber often used at the beginning of speeches and presentations.

Types of Grabbers

The best Grabbers to reach the OLD BRAIN can be classified into five specific categories:

1. **Mini-dramas:** a painful day in the life of your prospect contrasted with the benefits of your solution

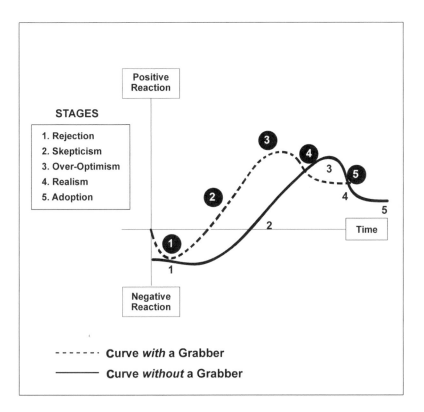

Figure 7.2 - Reaction to a New Idea

2. **Wordplays:** creative use of language gets attention

3. **Rhetorical Questions:** let the OLD BRAIN produce the answer you want

4. **Props:** using an object that symbolizes what your solution could do for your prospect

5. **Stories:** the OLD BRAIN responds to stories

So let's now review each category.

Grabber 1: Mini-dramas

"When you sell fire-extinguishers, open with the fire."

-- David Ogilvy, Advertising Expert

A mini-drama is a reenactment of a "day in the life" of your prospect without the benefit of your product or service. It makes your prospect relive the PAIN he experiences every day because he is not using your product or service.

The most effective mini-dramas close with a second act: a reenactment of the same situation with the benefit of your product or service. A sharp *contrast* helps the prospect experience the difference... and it stimulates the OLD BRAIN, which is very sensitive to *contrast*.

Here's an example of a mini-drama one woman, Agnes Perrot, used to sell herself during a job interview.

Agnes requested my help to prepare for a job interview. Agnes was a successful professional with an engineering background and a great personality. She had worked supporting sales engineers with a technology company for the past four years, but she wanted a job with a higher salary, more responsibility, and travel.

Agnes was applying to a hot Internet company in the process of expanding its international operations in Latin America. They wanted somebody based in the San Francisco headquarters to help their distributors with all pre-and-post-sales issues. The job required a strong technical background and a capacity to interact with prospects--in this case, mostly distributors.

Agnes had customized her résumé to fit the job description. She had already been to a first interview with the HR department and to a second interview with the recruiting Director. They had told her that she was one of the final three candidates for the job.

Although the interviewers expressed complete confidence in Agnes' technical knowledge, they mentioned some concerns about her sales skills. To dissipate this objection, they asked Agnes to come and give a 20-minute presentation on the subject of why they should hire her.

When Agnes called me, she was both excited about the opportunity and scared about the next step of the recruiting process. We met late on a Friday to prepare for her Tuesday appointment.

We first discussed the PAIN her future employer was experiencing: the reason why they were recruiting. She said that they were growing quickly, but their Latin American distributors were complaining about a poor level of responsiveness, a lack of proper communication, some missed commitments due to time difference and language issues, and the inability to get timely and accurate technical responses.

Then we explored what was unique about Agnes. What could she present to the recruiting people that no other candidate could claim? On the technical side, she already knew that her skills were a great match for the job, so most likely, this would be one of her unique CLAIMS.

Agnes was also fluent in Spanish. Although the other candidates may also claim to speak Spanish, Agnes' mastery of the language and her knowledge and understanding of the culture could become another valuable CLAIM.

Next, we discussed how Agnes could prove the GAIN she could bring to her prospective employer. Agnes had a number of interest-

ing stories from her previous job experience where she really had made a difference. She had helped closed at least two multi-million dollar deals, so she had a great example to prove her financial value. She had similar customer stories that would prove her strategic GAIN as well.

Then, because of her internal responsiveness and technical abilities, Agnes had some strong references from her previous management. These could demonstrate some personal GAIN for her co-workers or her customers they would not have to worry about getting the wrong answers from her, or worse, no answer at all.

Finally, we talked about how Agnes could present with maximum impact. We needed a strong Grabber. Agnes had never done a mini-drama before and even the word 'mini-drama' made her feel uncomfortable: she believed she had no talent for acting. However, during the course of our interaction, she gradually became convinced that this particular type of Grabber could have huge impact, so she agreed to try.

Here is what happened:

Agnes arrived promptly at her Tuesday appointment. After a friendly greeting, they invited her to begin her presentation.

They were evidently expecting her to use a PowerPoint presentation since a projector was already set up and available on the table. Ignoring it, Agnes said, "Let's take a look at the life of your distributors today. Imagine it's 6:00 pm on a Friday, and Marco, your Venezuelan distributor has a problem with the software. He has an important demo with a large prospect on Monday."

Here, Agnes picks up her portable phone. Speaking in the phone as if she were Marco, she pretends she is desperately trying to reach somebody at the supplier's San Francisco office. After several tries *and transfers, Agnes--playing Marco--finally manages to get a live person on the phone.*

Marco's English is far from fluent, so Agnes imitates Marco by mixing both Spanish and English as she tries to get her issue solved with the person she has finally reached on the phone.

In the mini-drama, Marco gets disconnected, so Agnes desperately dials again, playing on the frustration and desperation Marcos is experiencing at this point in his interaction with the company. By now it's 6:30 pm and when somebody finally picks up the phone again, it's someone in the sales department who cannot be of any assistance to Marco. It never occurs or seems to matter to anyone in the supplier's office that it was now 10:30 pm in Caracas and that they are going to miss the biggest opportunity yet in Venezuela because nobody is available to help Marco.

Finally, having demonstrated Marco's aggravation to a very painful point, Agnes hangs up the call with a grim look on her face, signifying the results of her desperate efforts to find a solution to the problem.

After a dramatic pause, Agnes walked slowly to the other side of the room and said, "Now, let's see what would happen to Marco if you hired somebody like me."

Once again, Agnes picked up her cellular phone, ostensibly dialing from Caracas on a Friday night at 10:00 pm local time. Instead of calling the central number at the San Francisco supplier's office, she--still acting as Marco--dials the direct line for Agnes Perrot, the newly hired technical contact for South America.

Agnes, speaking as Marco: "Hello, Agnes, es Marco de Caracas, como estas?"

Agnes, speaking as herself: "Muy bien, Marco , y tu?"

Marco: "Tengo un problema con el software..."

Agnès: "Si entiendo. Es porque…"

Agnes switches her phone from her left hand signaling Marco, to her right signaling herself. Also she uses a different voice to make it clear when 'Marco' is speaking. Occasionally, Agnes blocks the phone with her hand to explain to the three people in the room what is happening as she conducts the call in Spanish. Agnes explains to her audience that the deal Marco is working on is for about 500 licenses, the largest deal for their company in South America so far. Agnes even offers to fly out to help Marco close the deal. It is obvious to everyone that Marco is having a much better experience now that Agnes is on board.

As the call ends, Marco is evidently very happy with the help and support he has received.

The final act of the drama unfolds when 'Marco' calls Agnes back on Monday evening to explain that his demo was such a huge success that the prospect is now talking about placing an order for 1,000 licenses. Because of the size of the deal, Marco is requesting the presence of Agnes for the next sales call where he hopes to close the deal.

After 'hanging up' from the final call, Agnes went back to her seat and asked her audience if they could see how the life of their distributors would be impacted if they were to hire somebody with both her technical and cultural skills. She had chosen her two unique CLAIMS as:

- *The right technical skills*
- *The right cultural skills*

The whole mini-drama lasted no more than three minutes and Agnes was anxious to move to the next part of her presentation where she would deliver the Proofs of GAIN of her two CLAIMS. However, at this point, something odd happened. The VP of Sales interrupted and asked Agnes if she would mind leaving the room for a few minutes so the three could have a private discussion. While she waited, Agnes was nervous: Had she overdone it? Did they feel her acting was unprofessional?

When they called her back a few minutes later, Agnes had pre-pared herself to hear the all-too-familiar, "Thank you. We'll let you know next week."

However, as Agnes reentered the room, the VP of Sales smiled at her warmly, "I have never seen a better demonstration of sales skills. What will it take to bring you on board?" The rest of the inter-view was focused on the job conditions, salary requirements, and logistics. Agnes was not even asked to finish her presentation. She was offered the position and given a handshake agreement on the spot. In three short minutes, Agnes had managed to convince the three of them that she was the right person for the job.

Agnes called me back about two weeks later after she signed the letter of employment. She was thrilled about her new job, and she was even more surprised and pleased that they had increased her compensation package over and above what she had asked for.

The Grabber Agnes used *contrasted* the PAIN experienced in the life of the customer *before* interacting with Agnes with the GAIN experienced in the life of the customer *after* interacting with her. The selling power of such a mini-drama was enough to convince three people at once that she was the best person for the job. It also managed to *prove* the GAIN of the CLAIMS she was making in three short minutes.

It took Agnes a complete weekend of brainstorming and several hours of rehearsal. At first, she admitted, she wasn't entirely com-fortable with her planned performance. But, retrospectively, Agnes now says it was the best investment of her time. A mini-drama is the most efficient way of impacting the OLD BRAIN. It focuses on the PAIN of the prospect, creating an *emotional* reaction and a strong, memorable event.

Panasonic even used a mini-drama in a print ad I came across recently. The ad was for Toughbook computers and proceeded to describe a situation where an individual, rushing to a pending presentation, accidentally dropped his laptop in the street. Reading the ad, I was caught up in the drama of the tale, and my heart plunged right along with the computer in the story as it tumbled to the ground. However, wonder of wonders, the laptop was undamaged and the hero was able to continue on his way with no further problem.

Mini-dramas are actually entertaining stories that are imbued with *emotion.* How can you turn a story into a mini-drama? If you were selling computers with a similar CLAIM to Toughbook's, you could drop the notebook during your presentation, making it seem to be an accident. Then, you could build on the PAIN by telling your audience you've probably broken the computer, lost all your data and cannot continue the presentation.

Once you get a reaction from your audience and make sure their OLD BRAINS are wide awake, you make your point about the GAIN they can experience with your solution, by saying something like, "Oh, I forgot this is a Brand X Indestructa computer, so everything is fine." This is a great Proof which *Demonstrates* the value of your product!

Grabber 2: Wordplays

Wordplays are attention-getters. Good Grabbers add another layer of meaning, typically humor or logic to the original content of a sentence. As such, they engage the whole brain: New, Middle, and OLD BRAIN.

Here are some good examples of wordplays:

- *"More bank for your buck."* In just five words, Wells Fargo bank emphasizes the fact that they'll offer you the best banking service (CLAIM) for little cost (Financial GAIN).

Other examples of wordplays as Grabbers

- *"Blue for a better airline?"* -- Jet Blue

- *"When News gets Broken, Blame Us"* -- ABC News:

Finding good wordplays can be difficult and often requires the assistance of an ad agency. Such Grabbers are effective in printed ads and other marketing collateral. (S*ee Figure 7.3*)

© 2001 Diageo PLC

Figure 7.3 - Using Wordplays

3. Rhetorical Questions

Because there are no guarantees that your prospect will actually listen to what you are saying, why not start by asking a question designed to impact your prospect's OLD BRAIN and force them to focus on finding the answer? Rhetorical questions also represent an easy, interesting way of providing important information such as numbers, figures, and statistics that otherwise may not be friendly to the OLD BRAIN.

3.1 "What if you...?" questions

Imagine you are selling pacemakers to hospitals, and you are making a presentation at a large medical conference. Assuming that the CLAIMS you wish to establish about your product are:

(1) long battery life

(2) small size

(3) easy installation

Here is how you could start your presentation by asking a few simple questions:

- *What if you* and your patients could rely on a pacemaker that would last for six years?

  (4-second pause)

- *What if you* could easily hide the device so it becomes totally invisible?

  (4-second pause)

- *What if you* could install it in less than four hours?

  (4-second pause)

Do you notice that by asking such questions you draw the reader or listener into an internal dialogue? In fact, your audience will start to think about the positive things that would happen in their lives if they had access to the benefits of your product.

The *financially*-driven doctor will think about how many more pacemakers he can implant monthly; the *medically*-driven doctor will think about the increased autonomy it provides to his patients or how much safer the procedure is; the *aesthetically*-driven doctor will think about the fact that the device is totally invisible.

Using this technique, you are not forcing the functions or features of your product onto the prospect; you are simply enabling them to visualize how the benefits would positively impact their lives.

To make these *"What if you...?"* questions most effective, it is important to:

- **Carefully choose** the questions to reflect on the benefits of your CLAIMS.

- **Make the question simple and short.** The rule is to ask a question that is shorter than one normal line of text.

- **Pause for at least four seconds** at the end of each question. Without a pause, your audience will not have enough time to think about the answer to that question.

- Use *"What if you...?"* **questions** to appeal to the personal, *self-centered* aspect of the OLD BRAIN.

"What if you...?" questions also have great impact as print ads. W Hotels created one that showed a couple enjoying the comforts of their hotel room *and* appealed to the *emotional* side of the OLD BRAIN, asking "What if you found true love?" You can't help but thinking about the GAIN you might enjoy from any well-crafted *"What if you...?"* question.

3.2 What do these words have in common?

One effective way to engage the OLD BRAIN of your audience is to start your presentation by writing down a series of words and asking, "What do these words and/or numbers have in common?"

One of my clients defined a new paradigm for developing complex software. The main benefit of his solution (an automatic, intelligent code generating system) was a dramatic decrease in software development costs: up to seven times less expensive than the existing process.

However, his prospects systematically underestimated their actual development costs because, at the beginning of a project, they couldn't really see all the different factors that would impact their bottom line. They were consistently unable to foresee how much it would take to complete a given project and did not understand the GAIN they would receive by using my client's solution.

To make prospects aware of this issue, my customer used the following Grabber:

"What do the following have in common?"

- Radio waves

- Magnetic field

- Black holes

- The future

- Hidden Software development costs

The answer? There is scientific evidence that they all exist even though they are not easily visible.

By making the connection between Software Development Costs and other abstract concepts, the prospects were able to change their perception of how substantial those costs really could be.

This paradigm shift allowed them to glimpse what benefits they would get by using my customer's software.

3.3 Number Play

Here's a similar type of rhetorical question called a number play. Sina Fahte, a CEO in the hardware industry, started a presentation to a small group of venture capitalists by asking the following:

"What do these numbers have in common?"

- 120
- 25
- 10 to 2
- 5 and 3
- 100

After a one-minute pause while the audience analyzed the situation, Sina completed the demonstration by saying, "These numbers represent the state of the wireless market and what we could do for it:

- 120 million is the number of wireless devices sold this year
- 25 is the annual percentage of growth of this market
- 10 dollars is the cost of our solution today--going down to 2 dollars over a 3-year period
- 5 is the number of granted patents we have already received with 3 more pending
- Finally, we project that our revenues will grow to 100 million dollars in 5 years."

The same numbers would typically be presented in a conventional corporate overview format which, though accepted by the

New Brain, is completely unfriendly and has little or no impact on the OLD BRAIN. However, by using a number play in the form of a Question, you make sure that your audience's OLD BRAIN doesn't fall asleep: it is a fast and effective way of presenting important numbers or words with impact.

Grabber 4: Props

Most of us love props because they are *tangible* and visual__and they often remind us of toys we had when we were kids. This attachment for simple, concrete objects or props is deeply rooted in our OLD BRAIN. Interestingly, recent research has proven that objects identified as 'tools' have the biggest impact on the OLD BRAIN. Using a prop in your presentation will ensure that your prospect will remember your message__Guaranteed!

Of course, the object you choose should have a powerful significance in the world of your prospect: it is not just intended as entertainment. You'll want to use a prop when you need your prospect to remember one of the benefits of your solution forever.

Here are some real life examples of how you could use a prop:

Natasha Deganello is head of Shabono, a firm specializing in Corporate Identities and Branding. One day, one of her prospects called to request a presentation of her portfolio. They needed to redesign their logo, recreate their brochure, and solidify their corporate identity. Her prospect was a mid-sized software company specializing in security software. Natasha

had reviewed all the collateral of her prospect and it was obvious that they needed to standardize their corporate image to make it consistent and cohesive.

Natasha met with the CEO, the V.P. of Marketing and the Director of Communication.

"Today, you have three different product lines," she said. "Each one deals with security. The first is a simple security encryption for small network applications. The second is for web-enabled applications, and the third consists of security products for large e-commerce applications that require commercial grade security.

So, to ensure that the software will not be broken into or stolen, you provide locks." Natasha pulled a large lock out of her bag and waved it in front of them as she continued, "The problem, however, is that each of your three divisions designs different locks." Natasha pulled a second and a third type of lock out of her bag. "No wonder you have a corporate identity issue," she said smoothly. "You are currently sending several different messages to your prospects, almost to the point of appearing to be several different companies."

She waved three very different types of locks in front of her executive audience. "I can help you look like one company, with similar locks, to meet your prospects' broad needs." With a flourish, she brought out three locks of different sizes but exactly the same model.

Natasha finished the presentation by showing off her portfolio as Proofs of GAIN to her prospect. A few days later, Natasha signed a contract. Per her suggestion, the company started buying small key chains with a lock that they leave behind every time they meet with a prospect.

Here is another example of the lasting impact a prop can have:

Back when I worked at Silicon Graphics, their logo was a 3D cube. In my capacity, I had to give many presentations about the company and their products: supercomputers, large graphics workstations, and servers.

Knowing the value of a good prop, I found an 8-inch cube that looked exactly like the Silicon Graphics logo and used it to explain how the graphics engine inside the machine processed geometrical information. This was a strong Claim for SGI, allowing the user to rotate, zoom in, pan, tilt, or even slice any object in any possible position.

The SGI hardware was very complex and few people really understood how the "geometry engine" worked. However, 100% of my prospects loved the prop because it helped them see how the SGI system worked and why it was unique.

One day, years later, as I walked through the airport in Munich, Germany, a stranger approached me saying, "You're the cube guy! You probably don't remember me, but I visited your headquarters about three years ago with a large group of German Executives and I remember your presentation with the cube. In fact, my company ended up placing a large order for SGI computers."

That's the power of using a prop: people will remember you and your presentation long after the impact of a traditional message normally fades away. The image of the prop will be forever stored in the long-term memory of their OLD BRAIN.

How to use props:

- **Use a prop when you want to illustrate a specific point** of your presentation__and make sure it's relevant. At the end of the day, it might be the only thing they remember about you.

- **Choose a prop that is appropriate** in the environment in which you are presenting. Using a pack of cigarettes as a prop during a lung cancer conference may be a bad idea... or it could get you a standing ovation. It all depends on the context and the audience.

- **Rehearse.** Just like a joke with a bad punch line, nothing would make you look more foolish than if your prop fails to illustrate your point. Looking back at the example of using locks as a prop for a presentation to a software security company, imagine the negative connotation to the OLD BRAIN if one of the locks accidentally popped open while you were using it to demonstrate the security and dependability of the solution!

Grabber 5: Stories

"The writer's job is to dig so much into his own story that he reaches everyone's story."

-- William Stafford, American Writer and Poet

I once heard a story originally told by Winston Churchill in the late 1930's. The objective was to convince the British Parliament to approve his request for a larger military budget. The increase was necessary to allow the development of new weapons. However, Churchill was facing opposition by a number of representatives who strongly rejected the idea of increasing the budget for new, unproven technologies. He told the story of the battle of Om-Durman as follows:

"Remember the war England fought in Africa in the late 1800's? Our troops were fighting the Whirling Dervishes. The Dervishes were strong and courageous soldiers, and although their only weapons were swords, we suffered heavy losses. We had only one-shot guns

back then.

Just imagine what it was like for one of our soldiers to fight that war: you've been in the desert for four months, and after yet another poor night of sleep, you wake up with a dry mouth and a burning thirst. It's going to be very hot again today and you are craving a good cup of tea. As the sun rises, you anxiously await a new wave of attacks by the Dervishes. You are hiding out in 6-foot trenches and the still air signifies a terrifying calm before the storm. The sun is turning the purple horizon into deep blood-red and you can't escape the memory of yesterday's battle where you lost 3 friends to violent deaths.

Suddenly, in the distance, you see those terrifying red turbans. As the battle begins, you panic during the endless 20 seconds it takes to reload your gun after each shot. That delay gives the Dervishes and their curved swords plenty of time to approach. By now, you have calculated your odds, and you know that for every Dervish that will die today, a British soldier will have to give his life.

This was the horrific reality of war until October 21, 1898. On that day, everything changed. Britain provided troops with the newly-introduced Gatlin gun, the first automatic weapon. It could fire hundreds of shots per minute. Thanks to the Gatlin Gun, during the final battle of Om-durman, only eight British soldiers died for hundreds of Dervishes who perished."

"And that's the benefit of keeping up with technology or thinking it will always be the same", added Churchill to conclude his story.

After Churchill's story, the parliament voted overwhelmingly to approve his proposal.

The impact of a good story is that it makes your OLD BRAIN believe that you have actually lived that story. Stories put the audience in a world of sensory impressions that make it impossible for the OLD BRAIN to differentiate between the reality and the story: The OLD BRAIN feels that it has lived through the experience even if it only heard it told.

What else makes stories so appealing to the OLD BRAIN? Can stories actually increase your ability to sell to the OLD BRAIN? Let's look at stories from another perspective.

What do the following people have in common?

- Parents
- Grandparents
- Relatives
- Friends
- Spiritual leaders

Answer: They all care about us and they have all told us stories at one time or another.

The subliminal message when you tell somebody a story is that you care for him or her. It opens up their OLD BRAIN to your message.

Think of it this way: let's imagine that I am one of your colleagues, sent into your office to pick up a document on Monday morning. If I don't know you personally, it is highly unlikely that either of us would tell the other a story about what we did over the weekend.

However, if we were friends, it is natural that we would feel comfortable relaying a detailed account of our respective weekends. Stories equal caring. All leaders have the ability to tell stories that motivate people to act. In *Leadership in Paradoxical Age*, author Noel Tichy rates the art of story telling as the number three criteria that makes leaders, third only to taking responsibility for the leadership training of others and developing teachable points of views in areas of ideas, values, and emotional energy.

Stories represent a powerful way of highlighting one of your benefits or one of your CLAIMS. They help you make a point without resistance or objections from your audience.

Do you remember the story of Agnes Perrot's job interview and how she conducted a mini-drama to create impact?

Stories can come from any source as long as you can tie them into the world of your prospect. They are a subtle but strong way to imprint an idea on the mind of your listener. Imagine the impact if that idea is one of your CLAIMS.

Telling stories is an art in which many business people have not been trained. Here are a few tips that make for good stories:

- **Make sure your story has a point** and make sure you make the connection for your audience. Don't rely on them to draw the connection on their own. A story with no point is like a joke with no punch line: it's a waste of time.

- **Make the story personal.** Don't say "A woman went to a job interview." Say "Agnes went to a job interview."

- **Put passion into your story.** Add details that prove you really lived or experienced that story. Create those sensory impressions that will impact the OLD BRAIN and help your prospects envision themselves in the story.

An effective way of using a story with a prospect is to tell a customer story. If you were presenting to Mercedes, for example, imagine the impact of using a story that illustrates what BMW gained by using your solution.

When telling a customer story, be sure to:

- **Include the company name** if confidentiality is not an issue. Also include the name of the key person who is featured in the story. This makes it more concrete for your listener.

- **Make it personal:** draw at least three parallels between the prospect in the story and the company you are presenting to.

- **Contrast what your prospect's life** was like *before* your product with their life *after* they started using your product.

- **Present specific, tangible benefits** instead of using generalities.

- **Highlight the GAIN:** Financial, Strategic, or Personal.

In fact, the stories are so important that we will discuss them later on in the book again.

Message Building Block #2: Big Picture

"A picture is worth a thousand words."

-- Unknown

An enormous body of research, particularly that of Dr. Joseph LeDoux, Director of Neuroscience at New York City University, has shown that, of all our senses, it is the *visual* input that reaches the OLD BRAIN fastest. The visual nerve carries information 25 times faster than the auditory nerve. In fact, neuroscientists have demonstrated that the OLD BRAIN registers images long before the New Brain can recognize or analyze them.

Technically, visual stimuli follow two simultaneous paths in the brain before reaching the visual cortex, an area located in back of the New Brain. One path, known as the "low path", traverses the OLD BRAIN to reach the visual cortex, while the second path, the "high path", remains in the New Brain.

Make a Strong First Impression by Creating a Powerful Grabber

In a very rare disease known as "blind vision", patients whose neurons on the visual path in the New Brain have been damaged cannot consciously recognize an object but they are still capable of detecting the existence or movement of that object as processed by their survival-oriented OLD BRAIN.

So what is the best way to add a visual component to your message so it goes directly to the decision-maker, your

we believe your laptop

should always last the length of your flight

and we go to hong kong

we put a plug in your seat for your laptop

so you won't deplete your battery

now you can keep on hold back from getting things done

especially when you have the time to do it

Canadian Airlines

Figure 7.4 - Big Picture

85

prospect's OLD BRAIN? A Big Picture.

Getting it at a Glance

Take a look at a Big Picture for an airline who discovered that one of the main areas of PAIN of their business travelers was the fact that the batteries on their portable computers typically ran out after one or two hours of runtime--consequently wasting valuable working time during long flights *(See Figure 7.4)*.

This ad qualifies as a Big Picture because it's a simple representation of how the airline's solution--a power plug for laptops--will impact the world of their prospects: even if you fall asleep in a Canadian Airlines' airplane, your computer will not run out of power.

Big Pictures are very important: as *visual* stimuli and they go directly to the OLD BRAIN. They also provide a canvas for more detailed information you may provide them later, thus accelerating the understanding of complex concepts.

Contrasted Big Pictures

Even more effective, *Contrasted Big Pictures* consist of *two* images: first, the life of the prospect is shown *without* your product or service and then it is shown *with* the benefit of your product or service. The first picture should clearly emphasize the PAIN while the second one illustrates the relief of the PAIN through the use of your product or solution.

We have all seen those traditional "Before and After" print ads with an overweight person on the left side and a picture of the same person weeks or months later after he or she has lost 50 pounds. We have seen similar *Contrasted Big Pictures* with balding men on the left side who display a full head of hair on the right side. This type of Big Picture--before/after, without/with--uses a very effective visual *contrast* that directly impacts the OLD BRAIN.

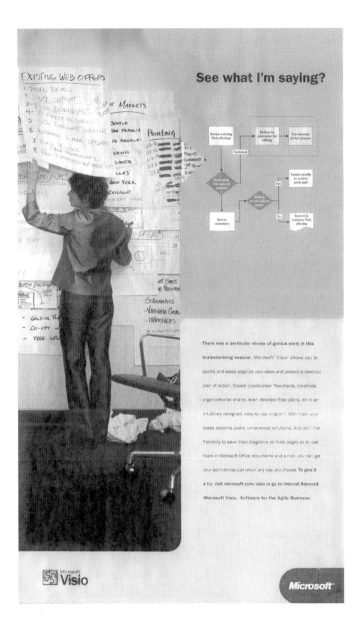

Figure 7.5 - Contrasted Big Picture

You'll remember that the OLD BRAIN prefers *contrast* so it can make a good decision quickly and easily. In a well-*contrasted* ad *(See Figure 7.5)*, Microsoft shows you the PAIN on the left side of the ad and the GAIN (or Relief) on the right side. Note how the visual *contrast* of the two images immediately enables you to understand the benefit of the solution regardless of how sophisticated or complex the product actually is.

In another example of a *Contrasted* Big Picture *(See Figure 7.6)*, notice how a fishing analogy is used to represent the world of recruiters. What if you were a recruiter looking for a very specific type of candidate? In this Big Picture, if you were specifically trying to catch a red spotted grouper fish, in which location would you rather fish? Does this ad illustrate the *contrast* of your world both with and without Careerbuilder? Can you feel the underlying PAIN of the individual fishing in the ocean? How long did it take you to understand the GAIN offered by Careerbuilder?

To maximize your impact, it is more effective to show the PAIN first and to portray the relief after. So the "Before" or "Without" image is usually on the left or on top and the "After" or "With" scenario is normally placed on the right or at the bottom as illustrated by the two ads above. This is because, in Western societies, the normal reading pattern is from left to right and from top to bottom. In other cultures, the order should be changed accordingly.

Now, let's review what you've learned about getting maximum attention from the OLD BRAIN. Always open your presentation with a strong Grabber using one or more of the five techniques:

1. **Mini-dramas**
2. **Wordplays**
3. **Rhetorical Questions**
4. **Props**
5. **Stories**

You have also created understanding for your prospect's OLD

Figure 7.6 - Contrasted Big Picture

BRAIN by delivering a Big Picture to help him or her visualize the benefits of your solution. Now, what are the other Building Blocks you need from your handy *Selling to the OLD BRAIN* toolbox to construct a powerful message?

You need to make your CLAIMS memorable.

Message Building Block #3: CLAIMS

"If you have an important point to make, don't be subtle or clever. Use a pile driver. Hit the point once. Then hit it again. Then hit it a third time --a tremendous whack."

-- Winston Churchill, Former British Prime Minister

In any presentation or message in any form, it is vital that your prospects leave with a solid understanding of your CLAIMS. CLAIMS are your key selling points: representing the actual value of your solution.

To help your prospects remember your CLAIMS, you need to make them short and relevant. It is vital that you repeat your CLAIMS frequently throughout your message to reinforce them. It is only when you express your CLAIMS simply and repeat them several times that your message will be easily remembered. The repetition of a few simple words sends a strong signal to the OLD BRAIN, prompting it to note, "I should remember that."

Effective selling of your unique CLAIMS will naturally disqualify your competitors, especially when your message includes several absolute Proofs supporting the GAIN provided by each one of your CLAIMS.

Make your CLAIMS Memorable by Repeating Them Again and Again

So, in summary, be sure to:

- **Wordsmith your CLAIMS** to make them the shortest and simplest possible. This really makes it easy for your prospect to remember them.

- **Keep your CLAIMS relevant** to your prospect: be sure your CLAIMS provide a cure to your prospect's PAIN.

- **Repeat your CLAIMS** so the OLD BRAIN bookmarks them as important.

> *"Tell your audience what you're going to tell them, tell them, then tell them what you told them."*
>
> *-- Unknown*

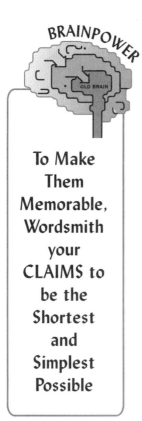

BRAINPOWER

To Make Them Memorable, Wordsmith your CLAIMS to be the Shortest and Simplest Possible

Clear CLAIMS help your prospects retain the core message of your presentation. By making them short, you will satisfy the OLD BRAIN's bias for *tangible* and simple information. As a result, your prospects will be able to memorize and repeat your CLAIMS consistently and accurately to other members both inside and outside the organization, thereby becoming your best active promoters and supporters.

In a conversation or presentation, you can signal your listeners that a CLAIM is coming up by using phrases like, *"The only thing you need to remember is..."* or *'Let me repeat..."* Keeping your CLAIMS short and easy to memorize minimizes the risk of distortion or miscommunication about your offering. **Following are some examples of effective CLAIMS.**

Not too long ago, Sprint PCS ran a print ad featuring a crystal image of a map of the United States with a cell phone engraved into the middle. The words "Free and Clear" were repeated four separate times on the one-page ad and the entire value proposition was developed around these two CLAIMS:

Free: you pay no roaming charges--a Financial Value

Clear: you get a crystal clear connection--a Personal Value

In the next ad (S*ee Figure 7.7*), Nationwide promotes three memorable CLAIMS: *"Speed, Simplicity, Savings."* Notice how they develop the value proposition under each one of those three CLAIMS, and how they repeat all three CLAIMS several times on the page so the OLD BRAIN is more likely to remember them.

Your CLAIMS are, in fact, the titles of the chapters of your story. They are the headings under which you should organize your Proofs of GAIN. They are the top reasons why your prospects should buy from you.

In a full-page ad published in a San Francisco newspaper (*See Figure 7.8*), "graffiti" is cleverly used to highlight the CLAIMS. Although it is always preferable to repeat your CLAIMS when time and space allow, the emphasis from the circles immediately leads you to understand the CarsDirect value proposition:

- *Save time (Personal GAIN)*
- *Save money (Financial GAIN)*
- *Get the car (Strategic GAIN)*

Cars Direct identified these as the three main frustrations of car buyers. The ad also focuses on the PAIN by reenacting the often drawn-out process of buying a new car. It appeals to readers as a story because it begins with the words, *"Once upon a time..."*

A message without CLAIMS is like a book without chapters.

Now you can feel

right at home

about getting a mortgage!

Whether you're a first-time homebuyer, you're ready to refinance, or you're shopping for your next home, Nationwide Advantage Mortgage℠ Company introduces a whole new way to finance your dreams. We're making mortgages fast and easy with our 10-minute mortgage approval. It's just one more way Nationwide is on your side.

What makes Nationwide Advantage Mortgage different from the rest? Take a look:

SPEED

Final approvals in minutes.
Unlike many other lenders who may <u>pre</u>-approve you quickly, but then put you through a lengthy final approval process, we make approvals quick and easy. Whether you submit your application online or by phone, you could have your approval decision in as little as 10 minutes!

SIMPLICITY

One approval includes different options.
You're also going to feel relaxed and right at home because we're not going to ask you to tell your life story. Our short application is surprisingly simple to save you time. We're also different from the rest in another important way. Most lenders will not even start the approval process until you decide on a type of loan. As a Nationwide customer, your approval comes with a list of all the products you have qualified for. So you only apply once, and then enjoy the flexibility of choosing from a variety of real loan options.

SAVINGS

Reduced or eliminated fees.
Compare us to other lenders and you'll find we've reduced or completely eliminated many of the typical costs associated with getting a mortgage. Many of our customers benefit from reduced closing costs like lower appraisal fees. Plus, with Nationwide you won't pay an origination fee!

If you have any questions, expert help is always just a phone call away. From approval through closing, count on the support of an experienced Nationwide Advantage Mortgage loan professional. We're here to answer any questions you have about the mortgage process, and we promise to make buying a new home or refinancing your current one easier than you ever thought possible.

SPEED. SIMPLICITY. SAVINGS.
That's the Nationwide Advantage.

Visit us online anytime at
NationwideAdvantage.com

Or call 1-888-244-8055
Monday through Friday, 7:00 a.m. - 10:00 p.m. ET
or Saturday, 9:30 a.m. - 6:00 p.m. ET

Nationwide
Advantage Mortgage℠

The Nationwide Advantage Mortgage solution is powered by Fannie Mae technology.

Figure 7.7 - Clear, Memorable CLAIMS

How do you expect people to remember something about your presentation if you do not make the conscious effort to create headlines and make these easily memorable?

Do you now have strong CLAIMS? Remember, "He who emphasizes everything, emphasizes nothing." Can you identify what the CLAIMS of this book are?

How about the 4 Steps:

- Diagnose the PAIN

- Differentiate your CLAIMS

- Demonstrate the GAIN

- Deliver to the OLD BRAIN

Note, from a mnemonic standpoint, how each CLAIM from *Selling to the OLD BRAIN* starts with a D and rhymes with the others. This makes them easier for your OLD BRAIN to remember. Just a note: if you have multiple CLAIMS, it is typically in your best interest to narrow it to three. Research shows that humans remember information more easily when it comes in sets of three, so your CLAIMS will be more memorable if you follow this advice. By using more than that, you may forfeit impact.

You may have noticed that we have broken our own rule by using *four* CLAIMS instead of a maximum of three as we suggested. Due to the length of our format--the book--and the amount of time we have to present our CLAIMS in detail, we feel comfortable using one additional CLAIM: we have the time and space to use *Grabbers* and visual images to back up our CLAIMS and keep your OLD BRAIN active and involved.

Ultimately, you will have to decide how to best Demonstrate the GAIN to your prospects using the time and methods you have at your disposal and how to customize your own CLAIMS to your target audience.

Your message should be constructed in the same manner: bulletpoint your CLAIMS and then build your presentation and proof for each one of them using a Grabber, stories, and Proofs of GAIN. along with all of the Impact Boosters that will keep your listener's OLD BRAIN awake and interested.

Figure 7.8 - Emphasizing CLAIMS

Message Building Block #4: Proofs of GAIN

Delivering *tangible* Proofs of the GAIN is where you should spend 70% of your selling effort! The core of your message should be your Proofs.

Don't waste your prospect's time by telling them something that holds no value for them. By sharing something that does not have concrete evidence to back it up, you are asking your prospects to make a huge leap of faith. Instead, provide them with strong evidence to back up your GAIN. Remember, your OLD BRAIN is very *self-centered*, so it only cares about its own benefit and it's going to be looking for some solid, *tangible* proof to bring it home with impact.

So, after presenting your Grabber, your Big Picture, and your CLAIMS, it's time to present your *Proofs* to back it all up. By communicating the type of GAIN you offer to your prospects--Financial, Strategic, or Personal--and the type of Proof you intend to use to illustrate it, you will become more effective in increasing your impact on the OLD BRAIN.

The best Proof of GAIN is a customer story--either testimonial or case study-- followed respectively, in declining strength, by a Demonstration, use of Data, and last, by a description of a Vision. Regardless of what technique you use to prove your GAIN, your objective should always be to:

Present Concrete Evidence to Gain Your Prospect's Confidence

- **Demonstrate the largest amount of GAIN**

- **Present the strongest Proof**

- **Creatively deliver the Proof** so it reaches the OLD BRAIN with impact

Let's now review the last two Message Building Blocks you need in order to deliver a powerful selling message: Handling Objections and Close.

Message Building Block #5: Handling Objections

Handling objections is a favorite topic in sales training. The objective is always to keep a positive connection with the prospects while still addressing their concerns. Objections should be addressed from the viewpoint of the true decision-maker, the OLD BRAIN.

Objections fall into two categories:

1) Misunderstandings

2) Valid objections

Handling Objections Resulting from Misunderstandings

Objections are often not rooted in logic. They are the visible part of how your prospect perceives you, your product, and your company. Imagine you are selling computer systems and you've done everything right: you've Diagnosed the PAIN, Differentiated your CLAIMS, and Demonstrated your Proofs of GAIN in a solid presentation using a fantastic Grabber, a Big Picture, and CLAIMS. Your selling effectiveness is off the charts and you're sure your prospect's OLD BRAIN is completely convinced.

However, just as you reach the end of your sales cycle, your prospect announces that although he is intrigued by your solution, he feels that the speed of the system you offer is not in par with some of your competitors. He insinuates that the level of performance would probably be within the acceptable range of their requirements, but that a faster solution would be more beneficial to their productivity and bottom line. The actual truth is that your system is as fast as any of your top competitors, but somewhere, somehow, the information was not conveyed properly. Such objections can typically be handled on a rational level by addressing the

New Brain. Here's how:

Step 1: Restate the Objection

Make sure that you understand the exact nature of the objection by paraphrasing your prospect's comment and openly asking, "Is this your concern?"

In the example above you could ask: "It seems like you need a system that provides a certain level of performance. Is speed your concern?"

Step 2: Step into the Objection

Your prospect's OLD BRAIN senses every symptom of fear you portray, however miniscule, especially if it is manifest in your body language. When faced with something our OLD BRAIN perceives as negative or threatening, such as an objection from a prospect, our natural inclination is to move away from the source of the threat. By moving toward rather than away from the person making the objection, you send a very strong message to their OLD BRAIN: you are not afraid of the objection.

Communication experts estimate that 55% of your impact comes from your body language. So, as far as your prospect's OLD BRAIN is concerned, your forward movement will be more important than anything you say.

Step 3: Hear your Prospect Out

Once you've stepped toward your prospect and acknowledged his objection, let him talk. Suspend judgment and practice true listening. As they say, "perception is reality", so if your prospect believes he is right, then he is, and you'll need to understand his point of view before you will overcome his objection.

Step 4: Deliver the Proof

Once your prospect has expressed his opinion, it is your turn to calmly and *tangibly* demonstrate your point of view. In the example above, you must show that the speed of the system you are selling is similar to or better than your competitors.

Tell a story, offer a customer testimonial, conduct a demo, or present the result of an independent benchmark or a matrix where you report the performance level of your main competitors. When you close on the objection, openly ask your prospect, "Did that help resolve your concern?"

The key in handling objections is to deliver a strong proof of your point of view in a manner the OLD BRAIN will relate to without discrediting the prospect in the process.

Handling Valid Objections

Valid objections are caused by your prospects' OLD BRAIN. They are triggered by the fear of making a wrong decision. Bringing up objections is typically the last step in the buying process. Therefore, you should welcome objections as a sign that your prospect is getting ready to make a purchasing decision. Unfortunately, objections also signal that the Proofs of GAIN you delivered were not strong enough and that your prospect's OLD BRAIN needs concrete reassurance that it will make a safe choice.

Let's take a look at a very common example of a valid objection: "The price is too high"

Being 'too expensive' is relative, of course. We all want to pay less for a product or service, but the reality is that we do not always end up buying the cheapest product.

For example, do you own the cheapest car, the cheapest TV, and the cheapest shoes you could find when you made the decision to buy? Most likely, you did not buy the cheapest option in every case; more likely, you bought the item that you needed and that provided you enough Proof of the GAIN you would get from purchasing it.

So, if your prospects object to your price, you should:

1) Make sure you have fully uncovered your value proposition or GAIN.

2) Revisit your Proofs and make sure they are stronger, more valuable, more *tangible*, and more personal.

Most often though, using pure logic to handle these objections is not enough. The OLD BRAIN is not purely rational and its reactions are based on fear, a highly *emotional* concept. Here is the most effective way to diffuse a valid objection: reframe it.

Step 1: Restate the Objection

As with an objection related to a misunderstanding and to avoid further confusion, make sure that you heard the objection correctly. Simply paraphrase your prospect and ask if this is his concern. For example, if your prospect objects to the price, you could say, "It seems that you need a system that will meet some strict financial objectives. Is this your concern?"

Step 2: Step into the Objection

Again, because the OLD BRAIN is so sensitive to fear, by moving forward you strongly signal that you are not afraid of the objection. It is necessary that this forward movement occur just after you hear the objection for the first time and as you restate your understanding of the objection.

Step 3: Wait for their feedback

Step 4: State your personal opinion

Because these objections have a lot to do with perception, agree or disagree with the objection by simply stating your own opinion. For example, if the objection is about price, you could say: "I understand that your concern at this point is about our pricing. Personally, I find that our prices are very competitive considering the value we offer."

Because the OLD BRAIN is self-centered, by stating your personal opinion, you make an OLD BRAIN to OLD BRAIN connection. You use the power of your credibility to convince your prospect to see your point of view from a new perspective. This is a good way to frame an objection, and although it is not usually enough to dissolve the objection entirely, it will help engage your prospect's OLD BRAIN.

Step 5: Present a Positive Side to the Objection

Most valid objections have a positive side. For example higher prices often translate to higher quality; late to market means that when the product is finally ready, it will be more robust; old technology often signifies reliability and dependability; and a slower product can mean a more secure solution. Whatever the objection, find the positive side that best counteracts it. Then, the key is to present that unique benefit so it goes directly to the OLD BRAIN. Remember, using a purely rational approach will not work. The best way is to tell your prospect a story, an analogy or a metaphor, that highlights the importance of the flip side of his objection.

You could tell your prospect the following story:

"That reminds me of a friend who needed a heart pacemaker and had to choose between two options: going to San Francisco State Hospital where he could receive a good pacemaker for about $5,000 or selecting Stanford Hospital where, for $10,000 more, he would receive the latest, most technologically-advanced pacemaker which would be implanted by the best heart surgeon in the nation. Which one do you think he chose?

Although you might find that our solution is a bit more expensive, we will give you the peace of mind of the most solid, the most reliable solution to your problem. When the health of your business is at stake, would you take any chances?"

If you counter an objection with a story or example, it doesn't necessarily mean that you will overcome that objection immediately or that your prospect will magically change his mind and buy your solution on the spot. If his objection was that the price was too high, most likely, he will continue to assume he can find a cheaper solution. But by giving him a snapshot of the Proof of GAIN, you offer a higher quality, risk free solution--his OLD BRAIN will begin to weigh your solution against the risk of an unknown or yet-to-be-discovered solution.

Since the unknown does affect the "survival" part of the brain, his OLD BRAIN will consider your offer very seriously. Your story will slowly but steadily work towards diffusing the objection.

Additional Recommendations on Handling Objections

You need to keep an ongoing list of the most common objections you receive on a day-to-day basis when you give a presentation or talk about your product or service. Because it is hard to find a reframe to every objection, and because it might take you a while to find a story that perfectly diffuses the objection, prepare a script for each of the main objections and practice delivering it-fine tuning it to achieve the best results.

BRAINPOWER

OLD BRAIN

'Reframe' an Objection by Presenting a Positive Side to it

Finally, the most important thing to remember about handling objections is that if you're put on the spot and can't come up with a good response, be sure and remember to move forward when you hear it. Your body language does speak louder than your words.

Message Building Block #6: Close

Many sales books suggest different types of closing techniques. If you have faithfully followed the Four Steps and have designed your message to impact the OLD BRAIN, there is no need for sophisticated closing techniques. It will be natural for your prospects to buy from you.

After all:

- Your prospect will have confirmed the source and intensity of the PAIN

- You will have differentiated your CLAIMS to show how your solution offers unique relief

- You will have demonstrated the GAIN they get from your CLAIMS

- You will have impacted the true decision-maker, the OLD BRAIN

The most effective closing technique for the OLD BRAIN is simply to do as follows:

- **Repeat your CLAIMS one final time.** *"In conclusion, we are the only company who guarantees you will:*
  - *Save time...*
  - *Save money...*
  - *Get the Car...*

Again, the OLD BRAIN remembers the *beginning and end*. This final repetition reminds the OLD BRAIN what is important that should be retained.

- **Ask for Positive Public Feedback:** *"What do you think?"*
- **Ask for the next step:** *"Where do we go from here?"*

Repeat your CLAIMS and Then Get 'Positive Public Feedback' to Close

Positive Public Feedback

Get Positive Public Feedback by simply asking, "What do you think?" and wait for an answer. If you have a large audience, direct the question to one individual. Asking for positive public feedback has two rewards:

1) When someone offers positive public feedback in front of a group, that person instantly becomes an active internal supporter.

2) Because that person will want to remain consistent with the public statement they made initially, their OLD BRAIN will always try to defend that initial positive position about you or your product.

Why does Positive Public Feedback work? Several researchers, including Dr Robert Cialdini, successful author and professor at Arizona State University, have demonstrated the importance of making a first small commitment which in turn triggers a larger commitment.

In a memorable study, Dr. Cialdini selected two identical neighborhoods to conduct an experiment. In neighborhood A, a select sample of households was asked if they would be willing to display a 6' x 8' billboard in their front yard in exchange for $100 per month. About 1% of the households said yes.

In neighborhood B, the same number of households was asked if they would be willing to display a postcard version of the billboard in their front window in exchange for $10 per month. 30% of the households agreed to proceed.

Several months later, in Neighborhood B, people who had

agreed to display the 'postcard', were asked if they would be willing to display the 6' x 8' billboard for exactly the same deal that was originally offered to Neighborhood A.

A full 25% of Neighborhood B, the 'postcard' group, agreed to display the large billboard in their yard. That means 25% of 30% (or 7.5%) agreed to display the billboard--a number that was 7.5 times more than the initial results from Neighborhood A.

Even if the public feedback you receive is negative initially, it provides you with an opportunity to address the objection in public. Chances are, if someone feels negative for any reason, they will talk about it with others when you are not around and you will not be present to overcome the objection. Sometimes entire sales are lost because the presenter did not explicitly address objections and assumptions when they had a chance.

The Law of Consistency

In the example above, when test subjects were asked to display the large billboard in their yard, they were naturally more inclined to do it than if they were asked to first display a small postcard in their window. It is easier for people to make a bigger commitment if they first made a smaller commitment. This is called the *Law of Consistency*--that is, once someone has made a first step in a particular direction, their OLD BRAIN will want to remain consistent with their original decision.

So your objective when you are asking your audience, "What do you think?" is to compel them to say something positive about your solution. If they do, it will be easier for them to take the next step toward a bigger commitment--like sending you a purchase order!

Next, ask, "Where do we go from here?" Again, let the prospect commit to it. If your prospect responds with "I guess we need to send you a team of three people to further evaluate your solution", it's totally different than if YOU suggest it.

Thanks to the *Law of Consistency,* if this kind of commitment comes from your prospect, that person becomes personally committed to making that meeting happen. At that point, your prospect or supporter will do whatever he or she can to assemble the team of three people and make sure they perform the evaluation.

WHAT TO REMEMBER

Each of the six Message Building Blocks has a huge effect on the OLD BRAIN. Let's review them once more:

*1. **Grabber**: Your opening attention getter*

*2. **Big Picture**: The use of a visual that speaks to the OLD BRAIN*

*3. **CLAIMS**: The repetition of unique reasons prospects should buy from you*

*4. **Proofs of GAIN**: Irrefutable evidence of what prospects will GAIN from your solution*

*5. **Handling Objections**: Being prepared for rational and not-so-rational objections*

*6. **Close**: Getting Positive Public Feedback and letting your prospects commit to the next steps.*

The Seven Impact Boosters

You can further boost the impact of each of these Message Building Blocks so they reach the OLD BRAIN even faster. Think of it this way: if the Message Building Blocks are the dishes on a restaurant menu, the Impact Boosters are the spices you sprinkle on any or all of them to make them more appealing. Use Impact Boosters!

1. Wording with "You"
2. Your Credibility
3. Emotions
4. Contrast
5. Varying Learning Styles
6. Stories
7. Less is More

Let's now look at the seven techniques that can tremendously enhance any and all of your Message Building Blocks.

Impact Booster #1: Wording with "You"

"A gossip is one who talks to you about others; a bore is one who talks to you about himself; and a brilliant conversationalist is one who talks to you about yourself."

-- Lisa Kirk, American Book Publicist

You know the old saying, "The way to a man's heart is through his stomach"? Well, the way to the OLD BRAIN is directly through the use of YOU.

The OLD BRAIN is *self-centered* and egotistical: that means your prospects don't care about your products. They only care about what your products can do for them. So, the best way you can help your prospects understand "what's in it for them" is to use or say the word YOU.

Messages Instantly Become Old-Brain-Friendly when Using 'You'

Don't say, "The new system will use 50% less energy than the current system."

Say: "YOU will save 50% on your energy bill with the new system."

Move away from the perspective of the seller and see yourself as the prospect. Ask yourself:

- Why should I as a prospect care about a specific feature of your product?

- How will I as a prospect really benefit from that feature?

- How does this feature contribute to reducing or eliminating my PAIN?

By wording with YOU, your prospect's OLD BRAIN will unconsciously experience owning and using your system. Your messages instantly become more personal and the prospect will feel you are genuinely interested in helping him or her solve their PAIN. Focusing on "You" beats focusing on Benefits--hands down, every time.

Most of us have been trained to sell the benefits instead of the features, but there is an even better way to communicate a point by using the word YOU in the process.

For example, if you were selling a copy machine, you could say:

- **Poor:** "This copier comes with a sorter and a stapler." These are features.

- **Better:** "This copier will save you time by offering a sorter and stapler." That's a benefit followed by the features.

- **Best:** "Don't waste your time sorting or stapling!" That can be a cure to one of their areas of PAIN.

If your prospect is pressed for time, this message goes to the OLD BRAIN faster than the others. It hits with a concrete, personal message that suggests strong Personal and Financial GAIN.

Impact Booster #2: Your Credibility

"Technique and technology are important. But adding trust is the issue of the decade."

-- Tom Peters, Author & Business Guru

Your Credibility Factor constitutes a significant portion of your selling effectiveness. Although it is a subjective and difficult value to measure, you always know it when you see it. In *You've Got to be Believed to be Heard,* Bert Decker, founder and president of San Francisco-based Decker Communications, maintains that it is probably the most important factor to maximize your impact.

"Your listeners won't care how much you know until they know how much you care."

-- Ken Blanchard, Author and Business Guru

Your Credibility is the core of what makes other people believe you. The OLD BRAIN is very sensitive to credibility because it conveys confidence or lack thereof.

Your Credibility is a function of six variables:
1. Your Creativity
2. Your Fearlessness
3. Your Passion
4. Your Integrity
5. Your Accessibility
6. Your Expressiveness

Credibility Variable #1: Your Creativity

"You won't be interesting unless you say things imaginatively, originally, freshly, creatively."

-- William Bernbach, Advertising Expert

When is the last time you felt you really used creativity to help other people understand you and differentiate you from your competition? How many times have you included a picture in the core of an email to break the monotony and help your reader understand your message *visually*?

Recently, our company, SalesBrain, helped a major high-tech company win a multi-million-dollar deal by applying the most daring business creativity.

A client of SalesBrain was bidding to be chosen as one of only three suppliers (from a field of 11) in a highly-visible international competition. The battle was fierce among all contenders.

Since thousands of pages of data containing product specifications and pricing tables for all bidders had already been delivered to the purchasing committee, we knew we needed a creative way to reach the OLD BRAINS of the decision-makers so our client's CLAIMS would be remembered.

Here's what happened: ten days before the decision deadline, we purchased a web domain name similar to the purchasing company's trade name and

Measure your 'Credibility Factor' in Order to Increase Your Selling Effectiveness

created an email address for its CEO. This way, emails coming from him at that domain name would be perceived to be authentic.

Then, we generated an email to all members of the purchasing committee seeming to come from their CEO. The email was dated 16 months in the future and congratulated each member of the buying committee for achieving tremendous success as a result of choosing the right vendor--SalesBrain's client--16 months before.

The email directed recipients to a web site where they could view a complete multi-media presentation about our client. This presentation highlighted the benefits achieved by the use of our client's system during the 16 months since the contract had supposedly been signed.

This was a very bold move. But less than 4 hours after we blasted the email, every member of the 26-member buying committee had opened the email and visited the site! The impact was phenomenal. Though some members were amazed by the fearlessness of our client, the message we sent was impossible to miss: our client was bold, creative, and committed to winning the business. Three months later, SalesBrain's client made the final cut as one of only three suppliers who landed the largest European contract in their industry.

The power of creativity is peerless but it takes a lot of work to be creative. Most of us recognize the benefits of being creative, yet we typically stick with established routine because we know it takes time and effort to be truly creative.

Luckily, there is a shortcut to creativity: it's called **variety**. By using variety, you will help the OLD BRAIN stay alert so your audience can be more open to your message.

Variety can be achieved by:

- **Including pictures, audio or video** segments whenever possible to stimulate the OLD BRAIN.

- **Varying colors in text or copy.** Colors affect your OLD BRAIN at a subconscious level *(See Figure 7.9)* according to Margaret Walch, Director of the Color Association of the United States.

Colors		
Color	Symbolizes	Used By
Red	Power, Activity, Rescue	Coca-Cola, Red Cross, Business 2.0
Pink	Calm, Feminism	Barbie, Pepto-Bismol, Mary Kay
Orange	Movement, Construction, Energy	Cingular Wireless, SalesBrain, Home Depot
Yellow	Light, Future, Philosophy	Kodak, National Geographic, Best Buy
Green	Money, Growth, Environment	John Deere, Starbucks, British Petroleum
Blue	Trust, Authority, Security	IBM, Microsoft, American Express
Purple	Royalty, Spirituality, New Age	Sun, Yahoo, Barney

Figure 7.9 - Color Chart from the American Color Society

- **Using a different medium than the status quo.** For example if all the other presenters are using software like PowerPoint, use a flip chart or tell a story or enact a mini-drama. Observe the impact of just being different from all the "me-too" competitors. You can be unique just by telling your message differently from everybody else.

Remember that all the effort you invest in being creative will translate into increased interest and attractiveness. This, in turn, translates immediately into an increase of your impact on the OLD BRAIN.

Credibility Variable #2: Your Fearlessness

"Be daring...assert integrity of purpose and imaginative vision against the play-it-safers."

-- Cecil Beaton, English Photographer

Have you ever noticed how small dogs often bark at big dogs but they rarely actually try to attack them? Why is that? Because the small dog's OLD BRAIN detects the absence of fear from the Big Dog, so bark as it might, a small dog will never purposely put itself in danger and actually take action to attack the bigger dog. Similarly, your prospects should not detect any trace of your fear...of losing their business!

Most decisions are based on fear.

The OLD BRAIN is the specialized organ for processing fear, a fact which is echoed by Rush Dozier in *Fear Itself.* "The primitive fear system (located in the OLD BRAIN) appears to be particularly attuned to detecting fear," states Dozier.

Be Fearless and Maintain Low Attachment to the Outcome

Imagine you are the purchasing manager of a large corporation. Your decision to sign a multi-million dollar deal will be based on your fear. You could lose your job or miss your quarterly bonus. It is that very fear that will trigger your decision.

Remember the old days when IBM mainframes were dominant? There was a saying, *"No one ever got fired for buying IBM."* IBM cultivated that image of safety which alleviated the fear their prospects had of unreliability.

The OLD BRAIN can detect signs of fear that are invisible to the eye. Did you know that customs officers are trained to read signs of fear in people who may be hiding illegal goods? It has been proven, for example, that the smell of sweat signals to the OLD BRAIN that a person is lying.

Also, as recently discovered by Dr Joseph LeDoux, "Our brains can detect danger before we even experience the feeling of being afraid. The brain also begins to initiate physical responses (heart palpitations, sweaty palms, muscle tension) before we become aware of an associated feeling of fear." Dr. LeDoux is recognized as having written the most comprehensive examination to date of how systems in the brain work in response to *emotions*, particularly fear.

Fearlessness might also be called non-attachment. By displaying an attitude of high intention but low attachment to the outcome, you send a strong message to your prospect's decision-maker--the OLD BRAIN--that you are motivated to win their business but that you have no fear of losing it.

To improve your fearlessness you should:

- **Act with high intention but low attachment.** Do your best and then don't worry about the immediate outcome. Although your OLD BRAIN might try to tell you otherwise, it is only business you are conducting. It is not a life-threatening event.

- **Keep a positive outlook.**

- **Remember that even the best and most brilliant people do not win 100% of the time.** However, those who are actively working on increasing their selling skills learn to harness their fears and transform the energy of the fear into something positive.

- **Practice, practice, practice.** If delivering your message includes public speaking, you will certainly experience some fear. In fact, in an extensive survey conducted by the London Sunday Times, statistics showed that most people are more afraid of speaking in public than they are of dying! Readers ranked their fears in order as follow: fear of public speaking was number one, followed by fear of heights, fear of insects, bugs and reptiles, fear of financial difficulties, fear of deep water, fear of sickness, and fear of death. So, you are not alone, and by practicing and rehearsing, you will not only improve the quality of your delivery to a public audience, but you will also slowly let go of your fear.

Credibility Variable #3: Your Passion

"Nothing great in the world has ever been accomplished without passion."

-- G. Hegel, German philosopher

Besides fame, what do the following people have in common?

- Pablo Picasso
- Albert Einstein
- Michael Jordan
- Martin Luther King
- Mother Theresa

Answer: They were all passionate about what they did.

Have you ever heard Einstein talk about physics or Martin Luther King speak about human rights?

These celebrities' passion for their work brought them to an unequaled level of excellence. Their passion could be sensed by anyone who came in contact with them.

In his book, *Leading Out Loud,* Terry Pearce writes, "I have often asked customers and friends to identify the most effective leaders they know and to look at the source of their power as communicators of messages. Invariably, names such as J.F. Kennedy, Martin Luther King Jr., Barbara Jordan, Winston Churchill, Mario Cuomo, and Ronald Reagan are mentioned. Certainly, these people had a command of their language, but as people point out, what stimulated others was neither the rhetoric nor the show; it was the conviction of the speaker, their energy, the passion for his or her cause, the extent to which that passion and that conviction were conveyed..."

In fact, recent research by Elaine Hatfield, professor of psychology, distinguished scientist, and author of a dozen books on human emotions, as well as research done by many other scientists has shown that emotion is contagious. If you are passionate, other people will become more enthusiastic. Passion is that intangible factor that you can sense without really knowing where it comes from. Passion is difficult, if not impossible, to fake, and, as with fear, your prospect's OLD BRAIN can sense your passion as accurately as your speedometer measures your speed.

Passionate people do not see obstacles; they see opportunities. They are not attached to the outcome; they enjoy doing what they are doing for the pleasure of doing it. Your passion can be detected in your words, your voice, and your body, and the best way to increase your passion is to be passionate about it!

Here are a few things you can do to maximize your passion:

- **Learn to measure your level of passion.** There may be a time of day when you are at your peak. For example, you may want to avoid making an important phone call with a prospect on a Monday morning if you had a major upset over the weekend. Your voice will not sound as self-confident as it normally would. Your best bet is to wait until later in the day when you have reestablished your natural level of passion.

- **Surround yourself with passionate people** because passion is contagious and builds on itself.

- **Practice and rehearse.** Although practicing and rehearsing will not impact your passion, it will increase your professionalism and it will decrease your nervousness both of which will help other people see you as a passionate person.

- **You can never be too passionate and passion is contagious.** If you are really enthusiastic about your product, your prospects will be too.

- **Do what you love and love what you do.** It will be easy for your audience to sense your passion.

Credibility Variable #4: Your Integrity

"To give real service you must add something which cannot be bought or measured with money. That is sincerity and integrity."

-- Douglas Adams, English novelist

How many customer relationships, how many personal relationships, have ended because one or more of the players did not tell the truth, the whole truth, and nothing but the truth?

Are you in your business for the long run? Do you care if you sell your prospect something he or she will not really benefit from? Will you be present when problems arise after the sale? Did you perform an honest diagnosis of your prospect's PAIN or did you hide a few things under the rug?

Meeting your commitments, making decisions that are based on what is good for your prospects, and walking your talk may all have an immediate cost for you, but they will serve you well in the long run. A number of large companies are devising careful mission statements just to define what it means to act with integrity.

Here are a few points about your integrity:

- **Don't fake it.** Just be you. Maybe you are a little shy and don't exude passion or perhaps you're not a very aggressive salesperson. That's perfectly acceptable. It's much better to be you and focus on your strengths than to pretend you are somebody else. Inconsistency, inappropriate body language, or misrepresentation can cause your prospect's

OLD BRAIN to go on the alert. It interprets inconsistency as possible danger.

- **Be honest.** Saying, "Sure, my system can do this or that," may be a shortcut to get an order, but lies often lead to self-destruction.

- **Know when to say "no" or "I don't know."** There will be times when admitting limitations or lack of knowledge will gain greater respect from your prospects.

Credibility Variable #5: Your Accessibility

"If you wish to persuade me, you must think my thoughts, feel my feelings, and speak my words."

-- Cicero, Roman Orator and Statesman

Let's face it, we all like people who are similar to us. Your OLD BRAIN is simply more open to people who look, sound, and act like

you do because it is able to relax its guard against the unknown or unpredictable. In fact, Rush Dozier points out in *Fear Itself* that the anxiety we feel regarding strangers could be an important element in the widespread fear of public speaking, since we tend *not* to be afraid to speak around our closest friends and family; even a large group of them. The trained salesperson knows the importance of being relaxed around others by being as relatable as possible.

A huge amount of research known as NeuroLinguistic Programming (NLP) demon-

To Be Trusted, Look, Feel and Sound Like Your Prospect's Best Friend

strates that highlighting similarities between yourself and your prospect makes your solution much more appealing.

NLP can be defined as the science of using the language of the mind to create more effective communication. It is an innovative approach enabling people to organize information and perceptions in ways that allow results once thought inconceivable. NLP is about modeling human excellence through specific techniques that allow an insight into the detailed mechanics of how people structure activities.

There are hundreds of studies that show that we like people who are similar to us and who are familiar. Here's an example of similarity in action.

A few years ago, I was working for John Metcalfe, an Executive at Silicon Graphics. John, was a seasoned salesperson who came with many years of experience in the field. John was more on the conservative side with nice, expensive dark Italian suits and a soft but persuasive voice. A Scot by origin, after many years of experience in corporate America, John had learned to wear a white shirt and a red tie with elegance.

That morning, the two of us were hosting the Dean of the University of Bombay, India--the largest university in the world--with a gigantic pool of exceedingly smart students and a decent budget for computers. This was an important meeting indeed.

John and I had agreed to meet 15 minutes early to discuss the objectives of the meeting and to review the agenda. When John walked in the door, I was shocked to see him wearing a brown suit and a striped blue tie. I have never been focused on fashion, but I suppressed the urge to make a wisecrack about

how unstylish and unattractive the color of his suit was. As John happened to be my boss, I refrained from commenting.

Minutes later, the Dean from the University of Bombay walked in. To my big surprise, he was wearing almost the exact same suit and tie as John! John introduced me to the Dean. John had met the Dean in Bombay previously and it was obvious that his rapport with the dean was very strong. The meeting went extremely well.

As it happened, as John and I debriefed after the meeting, John brought up the subject of his suit himself.

"What do you think of my suit?" he grinned. At the same time, I asked, "Did you notice the Dean had almost the exact same suit as you?"

John proceeded to tell me that he had met the Dean twice in India and each time, the Dean was wearing the same suit. So, John was inspired to dig in his garage to find a suit that our visitor could relate to.

A few months later, we closed a multi-million order with the University of Bombay. Obviously we did not win the deal just because John wore the same suit as the Dean, but I witnessed that John was able to establish a very high level of trust with the Dean... in just three short meetings.

When your prospect's OLD BRAIN perceives you as their *"best friend"* with little or no difference between the two of you, it relaxes and becomes more receptive to your message.

Here's another interesting example. Recently my wife, Nathalie, received a postcard mailer for DSL services offered by California's Pacific Bell. The card was addressed specifically to her and showed a picture of a confident, attractive, smiling woman drinking a cup of coffee.

The very same day, I personally received a similar postcard from the same company, but the picture on the front was that of a man sitting in a trendy chair with a slogan that implied I might be boring if I work too much.

Each postcard advertised the exact same product, but targeted different genders. Knowing that typically men will relate to men, and women will relate to other women, Pacific Bell created customized covers and messages and sent them to respective genders.

Pacific Bell knew that by customizing the ads to their target markets, their prospects would better relate to the message and therefore be more open to suggestions. Evidently, Pacific Bell recognized that the increased impact they would have on their prospect's OLD BRAIN far outweighed the cost of designing and printing two different ads .

Do you take the time to customize your message to fit the profile of your prospects? Or do you copy and paste your PowerPoint slides from a template with the hope that "one message fits all"?

To be relatable, align yourself with your target audience. It means tailoring your message so it addresses the specific PAIN of your target audience. It is easier to buy from people who look like you, sound like you, and talk to you as if they really know you and understand your PAIN... because your OLD BRAIN tells you to trust them.

Credibility Variable #6:
Your Expressiveness

"If I went back to college again, I'd concentrate on two areas: learning to write and to speak before an audience. Nothing in life is more important than the ability to communicate effectively."

-- *Gerald Ford, 38th US President*

When delivering your message in person, the quality of your ability to express yourself with impact is conveyed in three ways:

1. Your Words

2. Your Voice

3. Your Body Language

Several prominent communications specialists, including Professor Albert Mehrabian of UCLA, have demonstrated that in some cases the impact of our words can be as low as 7%, when 38% can come from your voice and 55% is achieved with your body language (*See Figure 7.10*).

In *Delivering Dynamic Presentations: Using Your Voice and Body for Impact*, Ralph Hillmann, Ph.D., Professor of Speech Communications, also demonstrates how your voice and body posture can make all the difference in how well your message is understood: from effective pitch patterns to the amazing impact of posture.

Expressiveness: Your Words

> *"The difference between 'almost the right word' and the 'right word' is the difference between a lighting bug and lighting."*
>
> *-- Mark Twain, American Author*

When you simply want to inform an audience, the written medium is best. Facts and information are efficiently transferred to others in writing, since, statistically, you read about five times faster than you speak. However, be aware that writing typically activates only rational thinking, handled by the New Brain--and not by the true decision-maker: the OLD BRAIN.

When you want to *persuade*--to move people to make decisions

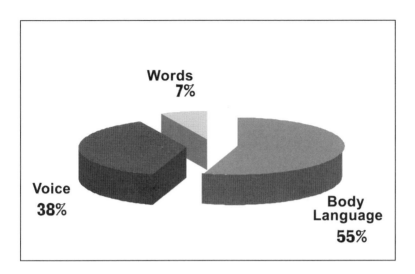

Words
7%

Voice
38%

Body
Language
55%

Figure 7.10 - The Source of Your Impact

and to take action--speak to them. Spoken information, especially when you are face-to-face, carries across your energy and passion and generates more *emotion* than written words do. It impacts the OLD BRAIN much more powerfully. **When it comes to your words, two rules apply:**

- **Your words must be carefully chosen.** Finding the exact words will help maximize the impact of your delivery.

- **It is vital that you minimize the number of written words you use,** especially when displayed on slides.

Be cautious of words, bad habits, or speech patterns that decrease your credibility:

It's Not
What You
Say; It's
How You
Say It That
Matters
Most

- **Avoid using words that your audience may not under stand** such as undefined acronyms or jargon that will not commonly be recognized by your listeners.

- **Avoid saying "I think", "I believe", "hopefully"**, or any expression that dilutes your message and your conviction. Avoid non-words like 'Uh,' and 'Umm' that are distracting as well.

- **Avoid complex sentences.** During World War II, U.S Defense authorities printed posters that read, "Illumination must be extinguished when premises are vacated." When seeing one of these for the first time, President Roosevelt exclaimed, "Damn, why can't they just say 'Put out the lights when you leave'?"

- **Avoid words that are too abstract** or that do not give a precise measure of a benefit. For example avoid saying, "We are a leading provider of..." or "We provide a flexible, integrated, scalable solution to..." It's not *tangible* enough for the OLD BRAIN to get a solid *visual* picture of the meaning.

- **Avoid repeating what's already written on your slide,** or worse, reading your slides word for word. Your audience can read faster than you and their focus will not be on you as you talk. Your slides should support your message, but they are not your message.

- **Avoid saying: "I will try to demonstrate..."** Either you *will* demonstrate it or you won't, but you should not *try* to...

To increase your Credibility Factor, *do* use:

- **Pauses.** Short silences help your audience process your information. They also help highlight an important point.

128

- **Simple, precise and concrete words.**

- **Specialized vocabulary used by your prospects.**
  Remember, the OLD BRAIN will open up to a 'best friend', so use the same words your prospects use.

- **Short and simple sentences.**

David Peoples, in his book, *Presentations Plus,* references a study done at Yale University which lists the twelve most persuasive words in the English language as:

1. You
2. Money
3. Save
4. New
5. Results
6. Easy
7. Health
8. Safety
9. Love
10. Discovery
11. Proven
12. Guarantee

And the most powerful combinations of words are:

1. Thank you
2. Would you please?
3. What do you think?
4. I am proud of you

No wonder wording with "You" is so effective!

Expressiveness: Your Voice

*"Surely whoever speaks to me in the right voice
him or her I shall follow."*

*-- Walt Whitman,
19th Century American Poet*

Is your voice as good as it can be as a selling tool? A study done at UCLA found that when speaking on the phone, 84% of your message is conveyed by the *music* of your voice, a combination of your pitch, tone, tempo and rhythm. Furthermore, brain researchers have discovered that the OLD BRAIN has highly-sensitive Credibility detectors. These detectors are pre-verbal, meaning they are activated by tone of voice and by body language, not by words. How often do you actively work on improving your voice so you have more impact on your prospect's OLD BRAIN?

The human voice is characterized by six parameters:
1. Pitch
2. Tone
3. Tempo
4. Rhythm
5. Emphasis
6. Pauses

What is the most effective voice to reach your audience's OLD BRAIN? We are all too familiar with people who are loud and/or who speak too quickly: these are not friendly to the OLD BRAIN which feels threatened when rushed or confronted with noise.

In fact the most effective voice to reach the OLD BRAIN is your *best friend* voice. When you use your best friend voice, you address your audience on an equal level and it maximizes your

Accessibility Factor: you avoid sounding like the stereotypical salesperson.

In *The Cluetrain Manifesto*, ranked one of *Business Week's* Top Ten books of 2000, authors Levine, Locke, Searles and Weinberger develop a powerful theory that the web is creating a gap between humans and corporations because of the difference of voice as explained by this extract from the book:

"Whether explaining or complaining, joking or serious, the human voice is unmistakably genuine. It can't be faked. Most corporations, on the other hand, only know how to talk in the soothing, humorless monotone of the mission statement, marketing brochure, and your-call-is-important-to-us busy signal. Same old tone, same old lies. No wonder networked markets have no respect for companies unable or unwilling to speak as they do. But learning to speak in a human voice is not some trick, nor will corporations convince us they are human with lip service about 'listening to customers'. They will only sound human when they empower real human beings to speak on their behalf."

When you speak to your "friends", you naturally vary your voice: your tone is deep and you pause frequently to think, emote, or emphasize a point. Pausing adds clarity and emphasis. Varying your voice reflects good energy and projects feeling.

If the message you are delivering involves your voice, tape yourself and listen. Then practice your best friend voice in front of a mirror and pretend you are giving this presentation to your closest buddies!

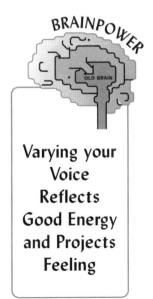

BRAINPOWER

Varying your Voice Reflects Good Energy and Projects Feeling

So whenever you present, speak to your audience, whether it's one person or 10,000 people, as if they were your best friends.

If you really want to improve your voice, ask your friends or colleagues what they think about your voice. Take the time to analyze it constructively; when is the last time you audio or videotaped yourself and carefully listened to your voice? Are you believable? Do you sound professorial, dry, or distant? Is your voice too high or airy? Do you say "uh" or "um" or "ya know" a lot? Do you speak too quickly? Do you effectively vary your voice like you would normally do when you are talking to your best friends?

Remember, your words account for only 7% of your impact while your voice accounts for at least 38%. Instead of spending hours wordsmithing a presentation, you may want to spend the time fine-tuning your voice for a mini-drama for maximum impact on your audience's OLD BRAIN.

Expressiveness: Your Body Language

"Stand tall. The difference between towering and cowering is totally a matter of inner posture. It's got nothing to do with height, it costs nothing and it's more fun."

-- Malcolm Forbes, American Publisher

How is it possible that some people are so much more believable than others even when they say the same words with the same voice?

The OLD BRAIN can quickly read your body language. Without even bringing this information to the conscious level, it will immediately disqualify or emphasize what you are trying to communicate.

There is huge amount of research and resources on the topic of body language. However, when it comes to managing body language, the most important habits that characterize people who sell to the OLD BRAIN are the following:

- **Maintain strong posture and purposeful movement.**
  For example imagine your hands drawing a large circle in front of you as you say, " You will be able to assemble large blocks of..." See how putting the emphasis on the word large at the same time as your hand movement really conveys a stronger meaning to the word "large."

- **Use gestures and facial expressions** to reflect energy and attitude. Do you know that of all the body clues you send to your audience, eye contact is the most important one?

- **Make sure you always remain facing your audience.**
  Turning your back, even for a moment, to the audience greatly diminishes your credibility factor. The OLD BRAIN will not hear what you are saying if it doesn't feel that it is being addressed personally. This happens easily when reading PowerPoint slides from a screen or writing on a flip chart or white board: prepare your visuals in advance or stand to the side of the board if you must.

- **Dress appropriately and be aligned with your listeners.**
  Just as it would feel awkward to appear in jeans and a T-shirt at a formal wedding, avoid looking radically different from your prospects. The key word is similarity, or what NLP experts commonly call "mirroring".

- **Use as much space as reasonably possible.** A common mistake people make when speaking in public is staying motionless behind a counter. It sends a signal that you are afraid of moving in front of the audience. When you take control of the stage and your audience's attention, your fearlessness greatly increases your Credibility Factor.

- **Involve the audience.** This includes asking the audience to move, to do or say things, to think, or to answer questions that may otherwise have been rhetorical.

Just as it is important to work on your voice, you will notice that practicing your body language is time well spent. Do not hesitate to videotape yourself and review your body language.

Check the following:

- **Is your body totally still or are you moving too much?** Too much movement, especially if the movements are not purposeful, or too much rigidity may send a signal that you lack confidence. Remember you should sound and look like the best friend of your audience.

- **Are you making any movements that are distracting** for the audience? You may be unconsciously touching your hair, tapping your pen, or jingling the change in your pockets.

- **Are you varying your voice and your body** attitudes to reflect your energy, your trustworthiness and to keep the OLD BRAINS of your audience awake?

Researchers such as Caroline Keating from Colgate University have established a correlation between common non-verbal gestures and the kind of emotions one is likely to encounter in business. In many instances, common gestures may indicate valuable information (See *Figure 7.11*).

In short you should:

- **Mirror the behavior of your audience**--including body posture, dress, appearance, voice, and even their words. All

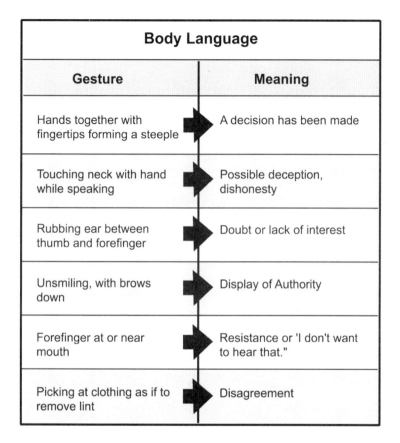

Body Language	
Gesture	**Meaning**
Hands together with fingertips forming a steeple	A decision has been made
Touching neck with hand while speaking	Possible deception, dishonesty
Rubbing ear between thumb and forefinger	Doubt or lack of interest
Unsmiling, with brows down	Display of Authority
Forefinger at or near mouth	Resistance or 'I don't want to hear that."
Picking at clothing as if to remove lint	Disagreement

Figure 7.11 - Body Language Interpreted

similarities help the OLD BRAIN identify you as a 'best friend' instead of a salesperson who has an agenda of his own.

- **Learn as much as you can about your prospects** or audience before delivering your message.

Body Language: Eye Contact

Although your audience will react to many aspects of your body

language, the most important is eye contact. When your eyes meet the eyes of your audience, your OLD BRAIN makes a direct connection. If your audience is made up of sev-

135

To Build Trust, Make Eye Contact for At Least 5 Seconds

eral people, it is important that you make eye contact with every one of them for at least 4 to 5 seconds. This will seem like a very long time, but this is what people naturally do when they converse with their best friends. When you are not making eye contact, the message you are sending is that you are not trustworthy. Regardless of what you say to your audience of decision-makers, their OLD BRAIN will not hear it.

Improper eye contact includes: staring at the back wall, staring at your feet or at the floor in front of you, making eye contact with only one or two people, breaking the eye contact in the middle of the sentence or in the middle of a thought and making eye contact for two seconds or less. Lack of appropriate, extended eye contact reduces your ability to conduct a "best friend discussion" with each person in the audience.

Here is a dramatic example of the value of eye contact adapted from *Integrity Selling* by Ron Willingham:

How Eye Contact Saved his Life

In the midst of the Vietnam War, a young American soldier named Robert and his platoon were pinned down in a bunker by enemy fire. Robert's fellow soldiers were all killed, and he himself was hit three times-in his right shoulder, his right thigh, and his left side.

Lying on the ground, weak and bloody Robert realized that, at any moment, he was going to die. He visualized his heart pumping all the blood out of his left side... and then stopping completely...

and then he'd be dead.

At that moment, some Vietcong soldiers arrived and started going through the dead American soldiers' bodies and taking their valuables-watches, rings, money, even knocking gold fillings out of their teeth.

Robert watched in panic as one of the soldiers made his way over to Robert, reached down for his watch, and discovered he was still alive. Immediately, the enemy soldier pointed his gun between Robert's eyes. This time, there was no doubt in his mind: Robert knew he was about to die.

In panic and despair, he looked up into the Vietcong soldier's eyes, and, with as much feeling and emotion as he could muster, shook his head vehemently from side to side and said: "No... no... please don't kill me!"

After several tense moments, the enemy soldier could no longer bear the emotional burden. Breaking eye contact, he put the gun to his side. Just then, another Vietcong soldier yelled something and the soldier responded.

Robert understood intuitively that the other soldier had asked if he were still alive and that the first soldier had answered in the affirmative. Then the other soldier yelled again. Robert assumed he yelled, "Kill him!" because once again the soldier pointed his gun at him and was about to pull the trigger.

Again, Robert looked deeply into the enemy's eyes, shook his head from side to side, and said, "No... no... please don't kill me, please don't!"

After an incredibly painful pause, even though he couldn't understand the language, the Vietcong soldier once again backed down, broke eye contact, and dropped his gun to his side. Then he did something amazing: he pointed the gun into the ground a few feet away from where Robert lay and pulled the trigger. He didn't look at Robert again. He yelled something to the other soldier, and walked away.

The one exception to the eye-contact rule: OLD BRAIN behavior is typically completely independent from our cultural backgrounds. In *How Customers Think*, Zaltman writes, "Consumers from very different cultures share a great deal and their commonalities outnumber their differences." That's because the OLD BRAIN comes from the evolutionary process of mankind and therefore follows the same practical laws regardless of our cultural or ethnic origins.

All the concepts presented in this book apply to and have been tested on audiences from countries as different from each other as Argentina, Australia, Belgium, Brazil, China, France, Germany, India, Indonesia, Italy, Japan, South Korea, the United Kingdom, Spain, the United States and many more.

However, the one exception to techniques used in *Selling to OLD BRAIN* relates to eye contact. In some Asian cultures, too much eye contact can be perceived as aggressive and disrespectful. Therefore, it is highly recommended that you inquire about local practices in specific cultures before applying the 4-second, direct eye-to-eye contact with your audience.

Summary

These presentation habits need to become second nature to you in order to reinforce your impact. Practice is absolutely critical. Practice until you don't even need to think about it. For example, your ability to establish eye contact for 4 or 5 seconds should become completely automatic so all of your energy can be used to deliver your message strongly and passionately.

WHAT TO REMEMBER

Your credibility is a crucial element of your overall impact. Though it is difficult to measure, credibility is found in 6 different factors:

1. Your Creativity: dare to be different
2. Your Fearlessness: demonstrate self-confidence
3. Your Passion: your enthusiasm will be contagious
4. Your Integrity: the only way to go
5. Your Accessibility: your audience must identify with you
6. Your Expressiveness: your words, voice, and body language must reinforce your message

Impact Booster #3: Contrast

What do you think would happen if you dropped a frog in a pot of hot water? It would immediately jump out. The transition or *contrast* between the comfort of the room temperature and the boiling water triggers an order to the frog's OLD BRAIN to take immediate action.

However, let's look at a different scenario. Take the same frog and drop it into lukewarm water. Now, turn the heat up under the pot and let the water warm up slowly. What happens? Often, nothing happens. The frog is content to stay in hot water--usually way beyond the temperature point that prompted the jump in the first experience--and sometimes it will even remain until its death. In this example, the absence of a sharp *contrast* between the cold and hot environment doesn't provide any trigger for the frog's OLD BRAIN to make a decision.

Sharp Contrast Helps Your Propect's OLD BRAIN Make a Decision More Quickly and Easily

That is exactly how our OLD BRAIN works : a sharp *contrast* will help our OLD BRAIN make a decision. So in a context of a selling situation, the absence of *contrast*, especially when prospects have difficulty understanding the differences between your product and others, will bring the ability to make a decision to a halt.

140

Have you ever been in downtown London when the temperature climbs above 75F? It sends hordes of businessmen out in the street without their shirts on! Yet the same temperature wouldn't create any unusual effect for people living in Florida. It's all relative--and it's all about *contrast*.

How much *contrast* do you have in your messages?

Trying to create *contrast* by simply using text documents or PowerPoint presentations is very difficult. However, mini-dramas, Contrasted Big Pictures, or stories can easily generate *contrast*.

Contrast often requires creativity. For example, you could show your prospect how life without your product is painful, complex, or expensive. Then you could *contrast* it with how painless, easy, or inexpensive life would be if they used your solution.

A few years back I was invited as a keynote speaker for a Linux conference in Korea. The room had over 2200 people and the speaker before me made a rather generic presentation. I noticed in the dim light of the room that the audience was starting to fall asleep.

After a short introduction by the master of ceremonies, I asked to have "the next slide please" of the total of four I was planning to use that day.

Then the fun began! Using a fake phone, I pretended my presentation was interrupted by a phone call from our IT (Information Technology) Director who had yet another problem with a major software vendor. Obviously I was not happy and while still on my call, I got into a serious argument with our IT director. I complained that the bug they had run into had been discovered three months before and that the vendor had promised to fix it, but that nothing had happened. Now, we had over 400 users who were unable to access their emails for more than 24 hours.

At this point, I covered the phone with my hand, and apologized to the crowd, who was still amazed that I had apparently interrupted my speech in front of thousands of people for a call about our IT system. When I 'ended' the call, I told my audience I knew they could relate because they had probably all had a similar experience at one time or another.

Then, changing my tone of voice to a more relaxed and deeper tone--to emphasize on the contrast--I said, "Let's imagine what your life would have been if you had been using Linux. How would the phone call have been different? The answer is: you wouldn't get an embarrassing phone call in front of a large audience. Why? Because your IT director would have reported the problem by posting a bug report on the web and, within a couple of hours, a Linux developer in the community would have had already emailed him a patch."

Suddenly I saw the audience relax. People were looking at each other and the room erupted in a wave of whispers as they discussed the situation amongst themselves. They understood that I was playing a mini-drama, and, more importantly, the contrast between the first situation and the second one helped them understand the message at an OLD BRAIN level.

Later, after many people from the audience came to tell me how they had enjoyed my little plot, I realized that the OLD BRAIN ignores frontiers. Contrast and any of the other techniques we describe to reach the OLD BRAIN work among all cultures.

So think of *contrast* as in:

- Before/After
- Without your Solution/With your Solution
- You/Your Competitors
- Now/Later

Positive *contrast* will move you from a negative situation to a better situation if you are talking about your solution. Negative *contrast* can be used to emphasize something painful about a situation, or if you want to undermine your competitors.

We have all seen the typical example of an ad with two images featuring a bald person on the left, the "before" picture, and the same person with a full head of hair on the right side, the "after" picture. This works because the OLD BRAIN "gets it" without effort.

Impact Booster #4: Emotion

"You've got to say it in such a way that people will feel it in their gut. Because if they don't feel it, nothing will happen."

-- William Bernbach, Advertising Guru

Many of us think that emotions are things that happen to us. In reality, according to Robert Cooper and Ayman Sawaf in their book, *Executive EQ*, emotions are an inner source of energy, information, and influence.

The very root of the word emotion is *motere*, from the Latin verb *to move* and the prefix *e* which connotes *move away*, suggesting that a tendency to act or to decide is implicit in every emotion. Thousands of years after the Romans defined the word for *emotion*, neuroscientists confirmed that only emotions trigger decisions.

Since *emotion* is one of the six stimuli that reaches the OLD BRAIN, the fastest way to influence your audience is through the heart, not the head. Whenever we experience a strong emotion, our brain creates a cocktail of hormones that acts as a memory maker and as a decision trigger. Rush Dozier, in *Fear Itself*, quotes, "The stronger our feelings, the more vivid and long lasting our memories... this applies to learning as well."

Dale Carnegie, renowned author of *How to Win Friends and Influence People,* said in his book, *Public Speaking*,  "When dealing with people, remember, you are not dealing with creatures of logic, but with creatures of emotion."

What are powerful memories for you? Driving a car for the very first time? Hearing about the birth or the death of someone dear to you? What you did the day of your graduation or your wedding?

Do you remember where you were on July 20, 1969, or on September 11, 2001? Likely you do, yet you probably do not remember what you ate for lunch yesterday. The *emotions* attached to a significant event are powerful memory-makers.

We are often surprised at how well we can recall vivid details of events that happened a long time ago. There is a scientifically-documented reason that our brains make memories: it's called *emotional* marking.

The cocktail of hormones that is released into our bloodstream when we have strong *emotional* reactions accelerates and intensifies the synaptic connections in our brain. If the *emotion* you felt was very intense like at a wedding, a birth, or a particularly emotional event, only one occurrence of the event is enough to create a lifelong memory.

I recently came across a visual ad from a software company similar to the one shown here (*See Figure 7.12*). This concept uses perspective as a Grabber to create powerful *emotion* in their prospects. Because the picture is taken from the perspective of a person travelling at high speed across rocky terrain, and because your OLD BRAIN is *self-centered*, your first tendency is to place yourself in the same position, causing you to feel as if you were also in a precarious position. This is a very good way to create an *emotional* and personal experience for the OLD BRAIN.

BRAINPOWER

OLD BRAIN

No Emotion, No Decision. Powerful Emotions Mark Your Old Brain and Reach Straight to Its Core

In the book, *The Emotional Brain*,

Figure 7.12 - Creating Emotion by Putting You in the Action

Joseph LeDoux explains how a baby in the womb experiences the same pounding heart and muscle tension his mother feels as she experiences fright if she slips and falls. The baby associates the feelings with fear of falling and later relives the same symptoms as an adult when the plane he is flying on experiences turbulence.

Using this concept, think how you might educate parents on the issue of kids using products like paints, glue solvents, or any other common home products as potential lethal drugs?

Study the ad targeting parents whose kids may have access to spray cans inside their homes *(See Figure 7.13)*. What kind of *emotion* does this picture generate in you? How long does it take you to understand the issue?

Emotions involve what we often call 'gut feeling', instinct, or intuition. Although many of us have been trained to follow our heads, dominated by our logical left brains, research has proven that we should be more willing to follow our hearts. There is a dramatic and distinct connection between our right brain, *emotion*, and the impact it can have on the OLD BRAIN.

In a revealing experiment, Antonio Damasio, head of neurology at the Iowa Carver College of Medicine, proved that the subconscious part of our OLD BRAIN becomes aware of critical facts before they actually reach our consciousness.

Damasio gave test subjects four decks of cards to choose from. They were asked to pick a card from any deck and then turn it over. Two decks were rigged to produce an overall loss--in play money--and two to produce a gain.

At intervals, the participants were asked what they thought was going on in the game. They were hooked up to sensors similar to those used in lie-detector machines to measure skin conductance responses (SCRs).

By the time the test subjects turned over about 10 cards, they began showing a measurable, physical reaction in the form of

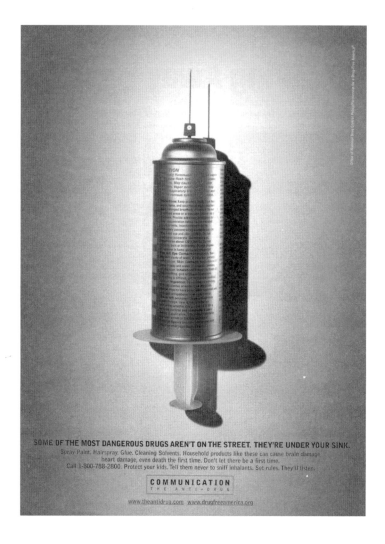

Figure 7.13 - Generating Emotions through Print Ads

SCRs whenever they reached for a losing deck. But, not until they had turned, on average, 30 cards, could subjects verbalize their "hunch" that two of the decks were riskier. It took 20 more cards, or a total of 50, before they could explain why their hunch was right.

Some players were never able to put their hunches into words, yet they, too, showed elevated SCRs, and picked more often from the decks that provided more rewards. Even if they couldn't explain it, their OLD BRAINS had detected the two decks that were favorable.

Now think about some of your past presentations or messages. Did you communicate at a purely rational level or did you instill some *emotions* in your audience?

Evaluate the amount of *emotion* in your usual presentations and in your messages. Then, pretend you are a prospect. Would you feel compelled to act or to remember the presentation beyond a few hours or days?

Creating an emotional message is not always easy, but if you follow the guidelines of *Selling to the OLD BRAIN*, your presentations will naturally generate *emotions*: for instance, doing a *mini-drama* showing the life of a prospect before and after your solution will automatically trigger a strong *emotional* response.

Impact Booster #5:
Varying Learning Styles

"A wise teacher makes learning a joy."

-- *Traditional English Proverb*

Peter Drucker, a preeminent business philosopher, has pointed out that one of the most important things you can learn about yourself is your information-gathering style.

Some people like to *hear* information. Some like to see the Big Picture before knowing the details. Some like to 'sleep on' new information before making a move. Some need to feel an experience to better understand.

In fact, people use three different channels to learn:

1. The **Visual** channel depends on seeing in order to learn

2. The **auditory** channel relies on hearing to learn

3. The **kinesthetic** channel uses touch

Let's do a test:

How many windows are there in your house or apartment?

Do you have the answer? What did you do to process the number you came up with? Chances are, you visualized your place and counted each of the windows. You had to enter a visual mode to retrieve the information: an auditory or kinesthetic mode simply wouldn't work. You will notice that this visual mode is indeed the native mode of the OLD BRAIN.

Let's review how the different learning channels are used:

The *Visual* channel is used with:

- pictures or graphics
- images and icons

- props
- the *visual* component of a video or a printed ad
- the *visual* component of a well-told story, mini-drama, or demo. For example, if you say, "I saw the sun rising on this new era", your listener is forced to go into his/her *visual* mode and "see" what you are describing. That is because you used the verb "saw".

The *Auditory* channel is used to interpret elements such as:

- any written text
- any spoken words
- the audio section of a movie or the legend in a picture
- the auditory portion of a well-told story. For example, if you say, "I *heard* the bell", then the auditory channel of your audience is stimulated.

The *Kinesthetic* channel is used:

- when people are asked to perform tasks or exercises which involves touching or experiencing objects
- with props
- in the kinesthetic portion of a good story or a mini-drama. For example, if you say, "The sun heated the asphalt until it was as hot as fire", it evokes the kinesthetic channel because heat can be experienced through touch.

***All three* channel** are used in:

- well-told stories
- well-acted mini-dramas
- demos in which the audience is involved

Although you use all three channels to learn, research shows that everyone has one channel that is more effective or more developed than the others. In fact, according to Genie Laborde, communication authority and author of *Influencing With Integrity*, statistically, 40% of people are primarily Visual, 20% are strongly Auditory, and 40% are Kinesthetically dominant when it comes to learning. So, you can see why it is vital to address all three learning channels every time you communicate to an audience.

Appealing to the dominant channel of a single prospect to get your point across is highly effective in influencing others. If you do not pay attention to your audience's preferences, you may throw away your opportunity to make impact. For example, simply *talking* about a feature of your product to a *visual* prospect is about as effective as swimming against the current.

Today, many business or technical presentations primarily use the auditory channel. How many PowerPoint presentations have you seen that squeeze sentence after sentence onto each slide? How many times have you been bored to death with a speaker who rambles without giving a demo, sharing a story, or presenting a strong *visual?*

Most Messages are Auditory. Make Them More Visual and Kinesthetic

It is critical to integrate elements of all three learning channels into the delivery of your presentation:

• so you do not neglect those in your audience who favor a different learning channel

• because using multiple channels helps the OLD BRAIN stay alert

Technology companies in particular have a strong tendency to sell their solutions using only the auditory channel. Many people who are tech savvy tend to primarily use their New Brain, which is responsible for thinking and logic, and feel more comfortable explaining the solutions they sell in a linear, rational, feature-centric way.

The best way to keep your audience engaged and to make sure that a large majority of people understand your message is to vary your presentation in order to address all three learning styles. If you only make use of PowerPoint slides with lots of text, you technically limit your appeal to the *auditory* channel of your audience. This makes it more difficult for visual or kinesthetic learners to process and it is not an effective way to keep the OLD BRAIN awake.

Let's explore the concept further. Take the example of the Linux Open Source Model (*See Figure 7.14*). Can you determine which channel is used to convey the message, the visual channel or the auditory channel?

Most people think that a diagram like Figure 7.14 is *visual* and

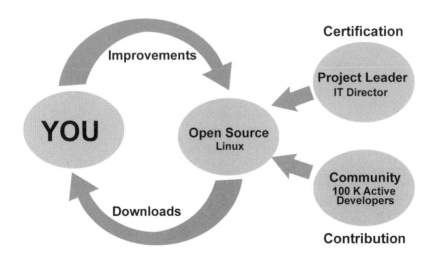

The Linux Open Source Model

Figure 7.14 - Auditory Information

therefore helps the *visual* learner. IT IS NOT! It is a better way of organizing written information, but because people have to read it in order to understand it, it cannot be learned through the *visual* channel. It is still primarily *Auditory*.

Now let's look at another example from the complex world of technology. This diagram (*See Figure 7.15*), although it does contain text, is primarily *visual*. The puzzle shape carries significance, which is best understood *visually*. You immediately comprehend how each element relates to each other via the connecting centerpiece. *Visual* supports make a huge impact on any audience.

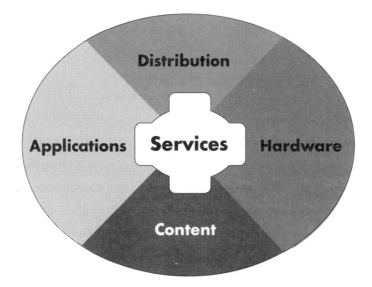

Figure 7.15 - Visual Information

Here are some Proofs of GAIN published by the 3M Meeting Management Institute for using *visual* supports to deliver powerful presentations :

- Retention increases from 14% to 38% when listeners see as well as listen to a presentation

- Group consensus is 21% higher in meeting with *visual* aids

- The time required to communicate a concept is reduced by 40% with the use of effective *visuals*

Printed ads primarily use the *visual* channel because advertisers know that images make a direct impact on the OLD BRAIN so people get your message much faster and more effectively.

When presenting, resist the impulse to *talk* about your solution or to simply list its features. Spend some time identifying powerful ways to make your presentations more visual or kinesthetic to keep the decision-maker, the OLD BRAIN, awake and informed.

Have you ever noticed that most clothing ads are highly *visual* and use little or no text? What is the PAIN of people who buy jeans? With so many choices, it comes down to the fact that they really just want to look 'cool'.

How do clothing ads prove the GAIN to their potential customers? The models in the ad are typically young, attractive, and hip. You respond because, thanks to a *visual* and concrete message, your primitive OLD BRAIN believes that you, too, can look or feel like the model who is wearing a pair of cool jeans if you buy their product.

Notice that clothing ads typically do not try to sell you on the quality of the fabric, the number of pockets, the copper rivets, or the zipper. They target what they know is the number-one PAIN: our desire to look cool. In a one-page ad, with limited space and time, a *visual* Grabber is the best way to get the attention of the OLD BRAIN.

In this ad for cellular phone service (*See Figure 7.16)*, Sprint visually demonstrates the GAIN provided by their new phones where users can literally *see* and send a visual response.

In another example, because their target audience is very spe-

Figure 7.16 - Visual Grabber

cific, note how an advertiser enhances a message by addressing a learning channel *other than* the visual one (*See Figure 7.17).

BMW discovered that a large number of their prospects belonged to a group known as Audiophiles: people who love music and demand very high fidelity systems. Undoubtedly, people who read stereo magazines tend to be more auditory. The *visual* in this ad shows a barrage of stereo speakers: *tangible* objects that the reader can easily identify with. Notice how the ad copy also appeals to the auditory channel.

Which Learning Channel do YOU Favor?

Let's take a simple test to figure out your preferred learning channel. First, just relax and take a deep breath. In a few moments, I'm going to give you a specific word. Try to remember the first thing that comes to your mind when you read the word. The word is...(turn the page):

Figure 7.17 - Targeting the Auditory Channel

bell

At first, did you: *hear* a bell? *see* a bell? *feel or touch* a bell? This simple exercise can give you your first clue as to which channel you favor most.

Now try this: read the following sentence and quickly count the number of 'f's it contains. When you are finished counting the 'f's, write down the number you found.

"It is only after a thorough evaluation of the prospect's PAIN that the astute seller will demonstrate the proven value of her uniqueness. She will do so with the impact of a Grabber that uses the 3 learning channels of her audience."

How many "f"s did you count? The correct answer is *five;* yet most *auditory* people will only find one. It typically takes auditory people several tries before they find all five "f"s because when they read the word "of", they hear the sound "ov", which does not include an "f".

In past presentations, have you equally used all three learning channels to reach your audience or did you only use the auditory channel?

Here are examples of what you can do to address the various learning styles, which will prevent the OLD BRAIN from sinking to the bottom of the attention/retention curve:

- **Tell stories.** Stories are conveyed with words, yet when well-told, they create sensory impressions that use all three learning channels. The OLD BRAIN is made to believe that the story really happened to him/her.

- **Use good *visuals*.** Look at your slides. Are they just a repeat of what you are saying, or even worse, are you just reading them? Or, are they creating a higher level of understanding by providing real *visual* information?

- **Involve the audience,** make them participate: it will make them use their kinesthetic channel. Ask them questions, have them raise their hands if they agree or disagree, let them talk, create exercises, let them touch an object such as a prop, or let them perform a demo themselves. Give them positive reinforcement when they participate. All this will appeal to their kinesthetic channel and ultimately their OLD BRAIN.

Another way to involve the different styles is to use words that evoke each channel. For instance, "Do you *see* what I mean?" works great for a visual person. "I *hear* you." works better for an auditory, and "It *feels* good, doesn't it?" is effective for kinesthetic learners. Vary your language to keep the OLD BRAIN awake in addition to using props or *visuals*.

One word of advice: do you remember the best question you should ask to receive Positive Public Feedback during your Close? "What do you think?" You will notice that this sentence is very neutral and doesn't favor any particular learning channel. You wouldn't want to ask, "Do you see the benefits of our solution?" to a prospect who is primarily auditory.

Impact Booster #6: Stories

"Persuasion always work better when the persuadee is not aware that he or she is being influenced."

Dr. Joseph LeDoux, Professor of Science, Center of Neural Science, NYU

Do you remember the different kinds of Grabbers like mini-dramas and wordplays? Stories also make for good Grabbers. In fact, stories are so effective that they should be mandatory in every presentation. If the delivery of your message involves some form of face-to-face communication, you should use stories as a strategic tool to influence your audience.

In addition to Grabbers, stories can and should be used in the development of your Message Building Blocks such as your Big Picture, your Proofs of GAIN, or Handling Objections. In fact, the best messages are those developed from beginning to end as a complete and compelling story. Stories are more influential than the best rational data.

But how is it possible that such an innocuous action as telling a story can have such tremendous effect on your audience?

Once again, it's a play for the OLD BRAIN. We are grown-up, rational people, yet when we see a movie, we often experience strong *emotions* which make us sad, mad, or even move us to tears. We know it's only fiction: 100% made in Hollywood. The hero didn't really die or that little kid did not lose his parents--yet we still cry. Our New Brain is well-aware that nothing bad really happened, yet the real Boss, the OLD BRAIN, with its primitive level of intelligence, does not differentiate between reality and a well-told story. Thus, the OLD BRAIN releases a flood of hormones that trigger our lachrymal glands and other physiological responses such as a tight

throat.

Good stories have more impact on the OLD BRAIN and our unconsciousness than any rational fact. The key to creating good stories is:

- **To create a world of sensory impressions** using *visual*, auditory and kinesthetic clues that will fool the OLD BRAIN in believing that what you told really happened.

- **To clearly connect the story you are telling** with the world of your client: why should they care?

- **To make sure your story really as a point** or a punch line.

So why is it so rare to hear good stories? "The real problem is that nobody knows how to tell a story. And what's worse, nobody knows that they don't know how to tell a story!" observes Jerry Weissman, an expert presenter and coach to CEOs of top companies like Inuit and Yahoo! in his book, *Presenting to Win: The Art of Telling Your Story.*

Remember that the OLD BRAIN is *visual* and though you may believe that your PowerPoint presentation represents a good story, the reality is that it often looks more like the Yellow Pages--a lot of text--rather than a good Hollywood movie that would please your audience.

If you have kids, you probably already know the difference between a good story and one that is not so good. If your kid

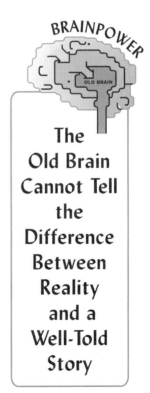

BRAINPOWER

The Old Brain Cannot Tell the Difference Between Reality and a Well-Told Story

leaves in the middle of your story, it's a good sign that you need to improve on your technique. The impact of a story depends on:

- **your content**
- **your delivery**

You have to excel in both if you really expect to compel listeners to buy from you today as opposed to tomorrow.

On the **content** side, this book provides you with a canvas to create your own story, starting with the PAIN of your audience, followed your unique CLAIMS and the supporting Proofs of GAIN. This content will have the maximum impact on your audience.

On the **delivery** side, your Credibility will add to the impact of your story. Notice how this book reviewed your Creativity, your Fearlessness, your Passion, your Integrity, your Accessibility and finally, your Expressiveness--words, voice, and body language--as the main areas that will reinforce or diminish your impact. In fact, the best stories are true stories that really happened either to you or someone close to you, because when you tell that story with the passion of an active witness, your story will become easily believable by your audience's OLD BRAIN.

Either you were born a great storyteller, or you can learn it. There are many good books that can help you there. Better yet, take a drama class.

Now, before we finish, let me tell you one last story:

One of our clients was preparing to deliver a compelling presentation to an international buying committee. The stakes were high: be on a short list of three selected vendors and win a contract valued at over $50 million dollars, or lose and see several million dollars of business a year disappear instantly.

When the company approached us, the executive team was

planning a standard technical "PowerPoint" presentation which, though it would make them look professional, would surely fail to make their presentation memorable or differentiate them from other, larger competitors. There was just one solution: design a presentation that would impact their prospects' OLD BRAINS: the PowerPoint had to go.

One senior account manager, Heinz, was an incredible individual whose charisma and extraordinary energy was simply not well-served by an illuminated screen with lots of text upstaging him. Though he had over 20 years of experience in the business closing hundreds of high-level deals using PowerPoint slides, we challenged him to give them up and tell a personal story instead--something that had nothing to do with technology--to deliver his vital points with maximum impact.

Heinz, a former two-time Karate world champion, rose to the occasion with incredible style. While most of the competitors for this deal were large billion-dollar companies involving multiple business segments, his company was the only one 100% focused on the line of products for which this bid was staged.

Beginning his newly-improved presentation, Heinz initially displayed the logos of his main competitors; then immediately turned off the computer and faced the audience. He explained that the main difference between the competition and his company was that the competitors were not focused on one business sector. So, regardless of their size, they did not have the same level of experience in one discipline and would never achieve the same effectiveness Heinz and his company could provide.

"When I teach Karate," Heinz began, "some of the students at the advanced levels start feeling pretty confident when they get their black belt. It's a very high level and it takes lots of hard work to get

there. So they look at me, the instructor, wearing my own black belt, and they start to make comparisons. They feel they've finally arrived and that now they're in the same league as the teachers. They take such pride in breaking boards or bricks with rapid and powerful hits, kicks, and punches."

"Now, there are several levels called 'dans' within the black belt itself," Heinz continued, "and what the kids don't know is that what separates a black belt at a high-level dan, say 7th or 8th which is world championship level, from someone who just got their black belt and is still at the 1st dan, is years and years of focus and experience. Literally thousands of hours of practice and focus have gone into achieving that experience and there is no shortcut that will get them to that level. Only years of effort, experience, and focus can do it.

The first exercise I give the students in my classes is not just to break a brick, but to break a brick with a one-inch punch. They are usually game at first, trying every way they can to break the brick by simply placing their fingertips on the brick and striking it as hard as they can. The problem is, with a one-inch punch, there's not much room to get momentum."

Heinz approached the table where the buying team sat and demonstrated the way to place the hand, vertically above the table, fingers pointing straight down with his fingertips resting lightly on the table.

Suddenly, catching everyone off guard, Heinz delivered a swift, extraordinarily-powerful impact to the table by quickly bending his fingers and making a fist which hit the table with a violent sound and alarming tremble.

"It's not just about having knowledge in a a particular field; it's not even just about the power of focus," he said. "It's about the

power of years of experience of working on one thing with tremendous focus."

The committee was still processing the rush of emotions as Heinz delivered his point. The presentation was to become the best the prospect committee saw, and they talked about it for months. After a series of carefully-thought-out and well-rehearsed events-- including powerful stories that would impact the OLD BRAIN, Heinz's company won the deal..

Tell stories. Good stories make a concept *visual* and *tangible*. They can make it personal, show *contrast,* and generate powerful *emotion.* In short, stories speak a powerful language that reaches the OLD BRAIN.

Impact Booster #7: Less is More

*"Let your discourse with
men of business be
short and comprehensive."*

-- George Washington, US President

Is there anything else you can do to maximize Your Selling Probability? The answer is yes: make your message shorter.

Imagine you are selling a product that has one hundred individual features. These one hundred features could easily be converted into 30 benefits, which, in turn, could cure ten of your prospects' PAIN. Isn't it obvious then that you should sell these ten cures?

NO! That was a trick question. You should focus only on the top three or even simply the number one benefit that would cure your prospect's number one PAIN. Why? Because your prospect's OLD BRAIN likes to keep it simple.

Your Survival Brain likes to see the best choice at a glance because time and energy required for analysis tends to cloud issues and slow things down. It tends to think thoughts like, "If I buy a product that is more complex, the probability that something will go wrong is higher. If this vendor is selling a solution that offers so many options, maybe I just need a simpler, less expensive solution."

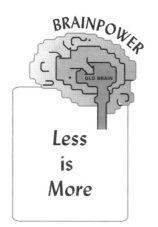

So, instead of giving your prospects all the reasons why they should buy from you, just focus your message on your one to three CLAIMS that address their top PAIN.

"Less is more" means you must remove anything from your message that has no direct value for your prospects. Make every element in your message count. Go for quality instead of quantity. Look at your message from the viewpoint of your prospects and ask yourself: "So what? Will this piece of information help me make a buying decision?" If the answer is no, remove it from your message.

Here is another important question to ask yourself: "Is the information I am giving absolutely necessary in order for my prospect to understand the bigger picture or in order for him or her to make a buying decision?"

Is the information you are providing needed for your prospect's decision to buy? If not, then you are *telling*, not selling. Telling is often necessary, but you should consider passing on training information in a written document that can be studied later, not in a face-to-face meeting or on the phone. Telling does NOT equal selling. Do not turn a selling event into a telling event!

If you apply the principles of Neuromarketing, you will quickly realize that, by simplifying the content, your existing messages and presentations can be delivered in about half of the time while your impact will increase tremendously.

Prospects will appreciate it if you only take 30 minutes of their time for a presentation that was supposed to last one hour, not to mention it may provide you with valuable time to handle objections before you go.

Review all your Message Building Blocks and condense your message until you can no longer remove anything without losing value. Don't be afraid to remove complete portions of your message if they don't pass the "So what?" test.

Recently, we coached one of our clients to fine-tune what was meant to be a two-hour presentation down to a very lean, but very powerful, forty minutes.

They resisted at first, feeling they should take advantage of the full two-hour time slot that was allotted to them-and not wanting to have less face time than the competing presentations. What they found in the long run was that after their absolutely fabulous forty minutes, the client spent the rest of the time just talking to them, providing feedback and information. It was, in the end, a much more valuable use of their time than talking "at" the client for the full two hours as their competitors did.

Best of all, their decision was validated when the client said, "Your presentation is the only one we wish had been longer."

Have you been guilty of overkill? Be honest. Neuromarketing: starts with attention to detail. Review and re-review every element in your message to make it as effective and tight as it can be.

WHAT TO REMEMBER

*To better, sell to the OLD BRAIN, you use the **7 Impact Boosters** to improve the effectiveness of your Message Building Blocks:*

1. Word with 'You': This permits your prospects to own your solution and prevents you from talking about your functions and features

2. Your Credibility: Your passion, your energy, and your conviction impact the OLD BRAIN of your audience

3. Contrast: Each building block can be enhanced by increasing the contrast-- before/after, without your solution/with your solution, etc.

4. Emotion: Prospects have a tendency to forget their problems are painful. Reenact the PAIN and make it personal.

5. Learning Styles: Most messages end up being only Auditory. Use the 2 other learning styles, visual and kinesthetic, to conserve the attention of your audience.

6. Stories: The OLD BRAIN can not distinguish between reality and a story well-told. Tell a story or use an analogy to more effectively influence your audience.

7. Less is More: Make each second, each object, each word essential to your message.

CHAPTER 8

PRACTICE, PRACTICE, PRACTICE

> ## *"No one has as much luck around the greens as one who practices a lot."*
> ### *-- Chi Chi Rodriguez, Professional Golfer*

You now have a powerful foundation and framework for a completely new way of looking at selling and influencing that is based on the newest brain research. It's interesting how the world's best salespeople and presenters practice many of these techniques intuitively, but now you know why it works: you're Selling to the true decision-maker, the OLD BRAIN.

The outline of what you need to work on is covered in the unique poster inserted in this book. Remembering and practicing the Four Steps of *Selling to the OLD BRAIN* will change the way you create and deliver convincing messages forever:

1. Diagnose the PAIN
2. Differentiate your CLAIMS
3. Demonstrate the GAIN
4. Deliver to the OLD BRAIN

Never forget that your Selling Probability is a combination of using the first three steps to create the content and then delivering with impact to the OLD BRAIN as shown in the equation:

$$\text{Your Selling Probability} = \text{Pain} \times \text{Claim} \times \text{Gain} \times (\textbf{OLD BRAIN})^3$$

Delivery skills are covered extensively in numerous sales and presentation books. However, none make the link with the science of the OLD BRAIN. To improve yourself, *see* yourself. Allow your own OLD BRAIN to respond to your own style.

The best way to practice is as follows:

- **Videotape yourself and self-evaluate your** impact on your own OLD BRAIN. Are you making eye contact? Is your body emphasizing your message? Is your voice convincing? Are you using the right words? You will not be able to get a good idea of your impact if you do not see and hear yourself as others see and hear you. *Remember:* your body language conveys much of your message. And since you can't see yourself while you are presenting, you should record yourself and observe your presentation critically. Work first on correcting your biggest weaknesses instead of spending time improving what are already your strengths.

- **Make a dry run of your presentation to one or two close colleagues.** Openly ask for their feedback. Second or third opinions are invaluable. Tell them your stories, perform your mini-dramas, and use a prop in front of them. Don't expect to get it right the first time. Redo it if necessary. Ask them if they feel that your Proofs of GAIN are unique and truly address your prospects' PAIN.

If you experience anxiety:

- **Mentally visualize yourself** giving the presentation and receiving a standing ovation. Making your visualization as vivid and packed with details as possible trains your OLD BRAIN to live the event several times beforehand. When you deliver in front of the real audience, your OLD BRAIN will feel that you've already experienced this many times and that it is not a threatening event that should generate any anxiety. Repeat this exercise for days or even weeks before the big event.

- **Practice deep breathing hours** or minutes before your presentation. By providing enough oxygen to your body, you will slow down your heartbeat. This, in turn, will signal your brain that everything is OK, and your symptoms of anxiety will gradually disappear.

Congratulations! You have finished leaning about the most effective ways to increase your impact in all your sales and communication events by activating the 'Buy Buttons' in your prospects' brains. Now that you are aware of this unique Neuromarketing model, you will not only enjoy the tremendous power of creating and delivering powerful messages that influence others, but you will also recognize how others can influence you by speaking to your own OLD BRAIN.

SELLING TO THE OLD BRAIN
IN EVERYDAY LIFE

This section describes how you can follow the 4 Steps in common yet critical everyday situations including:

Targeting your Prospects

Designing Print Ads

Producing Web Sites

Creating Emails

Leaving Voicemails

Delivering Speeches

Giving Presentations

Getting a Job

Targeting Your Prospects

Imagine you are looking at introducing a new product that can appeal to multiple groups of prospects. You need to focus on one group or cluster to maximize your chances of success. How can you best decide which cluster is the most likely to adopt your solution?

Step 1: Diagnose the PAIN

First, you should cluster your potential prospects in groups with similar PAIN. This may require extensive marketing research and great knowledge of your market. It can be very effective to do this as a team with the contributions of all relevant departments: marketing, sales, technical experts, PR, and executives. *Then, for each cluster, evaluate the PAIN factor as a number from 0 to 1.*

Step 2: Differentiate your CLAIMS

For each cluster choose and rate your CLAIMS. These CLAIMS should solve the main PAIN. *Rate them from 0 to 1.*

Step 3: Demonstrate the GAIN

For each cluster again you should now rate the proof factor of each of your value statements. Do you have strong customer stories with similar PAIN or can you use only some marketing data or your vision? *Rate your proofs with a factor from 0 to 1.*

Then calculate Your Cluster Attractiveness as:

Your Cluster Attractiveness = (PAIN) x (CLAIM) x (Proven GAIN)

The higher values of Cluster Attractiveness will indicate the low hanging fruit, those groups of prospects that will be easiest for you to close. Then for each cluster, evaluate its size either in number of prospects or in $ amount as shown in the table.

Then calculate Your Cluster Opportunity as:

Your Cluster Opportunity = (PAIN) x (CLAIM) x (Proven GAIN) x (Cluster Size)
or
Your Cluster Opportunity = (Your Cluster Attractiveness) x (Cluster Size)

In the following example (*See Figure 9.1*), we assumed the PAIN, the CLAIMS, the proven GAIN and the cluster size for each of the 4 clusters. Then, the Cluster Attractiveness and the Cluster Opportunity were calculated using the above formulas.

This approach gives you a simple way to combine the size and value of your market with your strength in each segment.

Marketing strategies often plan to go after the biggest cluster. Or they decide on target markets based on only some of your strengths. This can be a major strategic mistake, as it doesn't take into account other factors, such as the market resistance you may face in that cluster.

Your strategy will depend on your situation. In this example, if you were looking for your first customers, you might choose Cluster A where you have the strongest competitive position. If you

Cluster Attractiveness & Opportunity				
	Cluster A	Cluster B	Cluster C	Cluster D
PAIN	0.8	0.90	0.6	0.8
CLAIM	0.7	.90	.95	0.8
Proven GAIN	1	0.5	0.6	0.8
Your Cluster Attractiveness	0.56	0.405	0.342	0.512
Cluster Size in $M	50	100	150	120
Your Cluster Opportunity	28	40.5	51.3	61.44

Figure 9.1 - Clusters

were pressed by time and decided you wanted to close a small number of prospects quickly, then you should choose the cluster where your Cluster Attractiveness is the highest. In this case it would be cluster A.

If you were going after the biggest cluster, you would be targeting the prospects from Cluster C. The major issue with this choice is that although it might be a large potential market, it will be difficult for you to sell in that market with a cluster attractiveness of only 34.2%.

Deciding on your marketing focus only with the amount of PAIN of the various clusters would push you towards the prospects in cluster B. They might be more eager to buy, but would also lead you to difficulties. This might work for a mass market with shotgun advertising for a low priced product, but your *proven* GAIN in that market is only 0.5 and therefore Your Cluster Attractiveness and Your Cluster Opportunity in this cluster are both quite low.

The best long-term approach would be to choose cluster D, the cluster with your highest Cluster Opportunity.

This type of analysis gives you great strategic flexibility. You may pick different markets at different times in the product life cycle, or depending on your resources. But now you have a simple yet powerful tool to use for marketing decisions.

Your Print Ads

Step 1: Diagnose the PAIN

This should be done through appropriate marketing research, prospect interviews, and an effective analysis of your knowledge about the market. List the main areas of PAIN and then focus on the top PAIN.

In printed ads, 75% of your time should be spent on this step: if you assume the wrong PAIN, you will end up promoting the wrong GAIN to your prospects, effectively sabotaging the sale before it ever gets off the ground.

Since the headline is worth more than 50% of the power of a print ad, it should be a Grabber that deals with the PAIN and the relief brought by your solution.

Step 2: Differentiate your CLAIMS

Choose one CLAIM (or two, maximum), and then focus your entire message around the PAIN that can be cured by your specific CLAIM.

Step 3: Demonstrate the GAIN

This is the most difficult challenge in printed ads: to prove the value without using a lot of text. The proof of GAIN should be clearly illustrated in the picture.

Step 4: Deliver to the OLD BRAIN

This step is where you should spend most of the remaining 25% of your time. Creativity will be key. Printed ads are usually just a

Grabber or a Big Picture; on one single page, it is difficult to insert any additional Message Building Blocks. There simply isn't enough space.

A Big Picture is usually the most effective way to reach the OLD BRAIN because it is highly *visual.* When it links to a short, punchy headline, your impact is maximized. In fact, a picture used as a *Grabber* in a print ad often doubles as your diagnostic; the reader should feel that she or he identifies with his/her PAIN in that picture. Then, you can discuss or show relief to the PAIN that is portrayed.

When presenting your Big Picture, consider using *contrast.* Portray your prospects' lives as they exist without your product today, and then with your product tomorrow. Make sure about 80% of the ad is a picture: minimize the amount of text since people often don't take time to read. You'll only have a few seconds to get to their OLD BRAIN, so make it *visual!*

Be sure you are targeting the audience that will read that specific magazine or newspaper. Make the message totally tailored to the PAIN those readers have in common.

All examples of print ads featured in this book follow these rules. Two or three have even managed to add their CLAIMS. The Proof of GAIN is usually included in the Big Picture. Remember the CareerBuilder Network ad about a man trying to catch a Red Spotted Grouper fish? Often print ads do not develop their value proposition; they simply focus on grabbing your attention. Since it's difficult in a one-page ad to close the sale on the spot, their objective is to get you interested enough to take some sort of action such as calling for information or checking their web site.

In a print ad, you often have enough space to emphasize the prospect's PAIN. Make sure you are impacting the OLD BRAIN by making their current situation without your solution look painful!

Your Web Site
Step 1: Diagnose the PAIN

Here, again, you should know perfectly who your target audience is and what the objectives of your web site are.

Is the purpose of your web site to attract investors, to attract prospects, to attract new employees, or to motivate your current employees? The top PAIN of each of these targets is not the same.

Assuming the main objective is to attract prospects, it is important that you classify your prospects in groups that have similar PAIN. The OLD BRAIN is not interested in reading about somebody else's PAIN. Therefore, you may want to create different URL entry points in your web site depending on the prospects' main PAIN. If you find your prospects belong to three main clusters with distinct areas of PAIN, you may want to consider creating three distinct parts of your web site to address each group separately.

Step 2: Differentiate your CLAIMS

Choose two or three CLAIMS. Then for each cluster of prospects, focus all your messages around the PAIN that is related to these CLAIMS.

Step 3: Demonstrate the GAIN

Typically, a web site offers a good opportunity to develop your Proofs of GAIN. So, for each cluster, develop your value matrix and use the strongest proofs you can present. For example, using a customer case study along with a picture, and quoting your customer making a strong value statement will have great impact on the OLD BRAIN because it becomes *tangible* and personal.

A web site is versatile. You should use as little text as possible in your opening message. But you can provide links to pages of written details, pictures, sound, and so forth for those who want it. Include audio or video whenever possible and sprinkle in any new features provided by the latest versions of Internet browsers. Well-designed web sites are the one area of marketing where you can include infinite detail without boring people who only want the basics.

Step 4: Deliver to the OLD BRAIN

For each cluster, use a Grabber that makes your prospect re-experience their main PAIN. Use a Big Picture that *visually* shows how you will impact their world. Develop your CLAIMS and repeat them throughout your pages.

Go into the details of your Proofs of GAIN, making sure you don't talk about you and your company, but that you focus on how you can improve your prospects' life financially, strategically, and personally.

You will still want to provide a section of your web site that talks about you, but do not place this section ahead of the PAIN and your CLAIMS. Make it easy for your prospects to find the nuggets: do not bury your strong Proofs of GAIN under 20 clicks.

Your Emails
Step 1: Diagnose the PAIN

First, you need to obtain the name and exact function of the person you are trying to reach. Remember, the OLD BRAIN is very *self-centered*, so most people don't even read emails that look like a mass mailing.

A search engine like Google can give you background information on the industry, trade associations, and competitors. At your prospect's web site you can learn about the company so you can better assess the PAIN and customize your *Grabber*. Are they making their numbers? Did they go through any acquisitions or right-sizing? Did they launch a new product recently? What does the press say about them? How much of this really impacts the person you are trying to reach? For example, if you are contacting the VP of Sales and the company has not made its numbers for the last several quarters, be prepared to offer this person something that can increase their revenue!

Step 2: Differentiate your CLAIMS

At this point, you will most likely not need to state your CLAIMS. If you do start to introduce your CLAIMS this early in the process, make sure they are indeed unique and that you can back them up with strong Proofs of GAIN later.

Step 3: Demonstrate the GAIN

In a short email, you will not have many opportunities to prove the GAIN. However, the core of your message should be about the benefit of your product for them. In a Post Script, you also can include a quote from a prospect that gives you a strong testimonial for a GAIN statement. To further increase the impact of this email, you could creatively replace this quote with an audio, or even better, *visual* video clip of a customer giving their testimonial in person. Most email software now supports this feature. When you record the testimonial, make sure both the voice and body language convey a positive message.

Step 4: Deliver to the OLD BRAIN

Again, as in print ads, the time a prospect will give an email is extremely short. Your Grabber will be vital. You need a subject line that makes them want to open your email. Inside, you should also include a *visual* graphic: a Contrasted Big Picture would be best as long as it opens quickly in all browsers.

Because you have neither your voice nor your body to convey your energy, carefully choose every word you use. Make your message as personal as possible to appeal to the *self-centered* aspect of the OLD BRAIN. One simple thing you can do is copy and paste an image of their logo into the email.

Develop your Proofs of GAIN in as few words as possible and repeat your CLAIMS at least twice. Remember, less is more: make it half a page or less. Statistically, if the message doesn't fit within the screen, many people will not scroll to see what's remaining.

Close with a clear objective.

Example:

Let's assume you are trying a get an appointment for a one-hour meeting with an executive at a large software company called IBN (International Business Network). This person doesn't know you, but you are convinced they could use your product. You learn from their web site that their revenues are declining. You've heard through your network that the morale of the sales force is low. You have previously closed a sale with their main competitor, a company called GNS (Global Networking Solutions), and GNS has just reported a record quarter. Your product is a CRM (Customer Relation Management) tool and the name of your company is CloseProspects.

You can obtain their actual revenue curve and their logo from their web site. This is an easy way of making your message personal and introducing a short but effective financial value proof. Don't forget to use color in your text.

Look at the next page to see an example of an "OLD BRAIN-friendly" email you could write:

Dear Mr. Smith,

What if you could turn 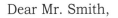 revenues from

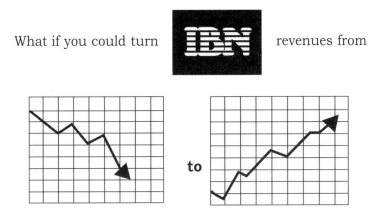

What if your sales force could close more deals and build relationships with your customers?

You will find that many software companies like yours have seen a significant jump in revenues immediately after implementing our CRM software. How? By:

- Closing more prospects
- Staying closer to their customers

Sharen Tilst, VP of Sales at GNS software, commented, *"With the new software from CloseProspects, our salespeople have closed 25% more business and our support people can finally claim that they truly are able to maintain close contact with our existing customers. Our satisfaction ratios have jumped 47%."*

If you want to increase your own sales and hear your customers singing your praises, call John Goodman at 555-1212.

With your success in mind,

John Goodman
CRM Expert
CloseProspects.com

Your Voicemails

Do you see voicemail as a "black hole"? Your messages go in and nothing comes out! Always be prepared to reach your target live, but if you don't, leave a powerful voicemail so you don't waste a golden opportunity.

Step 1: Diagnose the PAIN

Find as much as you can about the prospect before calling.

Step 2: Differentiate your CLAIMS

You do not need to state your CLAIMS as you will most likely not have enough time to state them... or the prospect will not remember them later.

Step 3: Demonstrate the GAIN

Make a short statement of your Proofs of GAIN. Depending on whom the voicemail is addressed to, a Financial GAIN statement might be the strongest.

Step 4: Deliver to the OLD BRAIN

Do not pick-up the phone before writing down what you will say! Prepare two scenarios:

- One for voicemail
- One for an actual live call if your prospect answers the phone

Typically, voicemails should be very short: 20 or 30 seconds, maximum. If you start your voicemail with your name and the prospect doesn't know you, you take the risk that they may erase the message before listening to the whole thing. In today's time-starved environment, many prospects do not have the time of day for what they may perceive to be yet another average sales call.

So, basically, you have time for a short *Grabber*, and a brief

Proof of GAIN. Close with your contact information. Less is more, so remove every unnecessary word.

Your only highlighter is your voice so practice, practice, practice before you actually call. Pay careful attention to your tone, the speed at which you talk, and the use of your "best friend" voice.

Using the same example as for the email above, here is what you could say using a short Financial Proof of GAIN:

"Mr. Smith, what if you could increase revenues by 25%? Yes, you can close more deals by building relationships with your customers. That is what happened at GNS. Three months after installing the CloseProspects CRM product, GNS reported a 12% profit increase while their customer satisfaction ratio jumped 47%. To find out how you, too, can achieve the same results, call me, John Goodman, at CloseProspects: 555-1212."

Here, again, you could greatly enhance the impact of this message if you played a prepared, short (10-second) audio testimonial from Sharen Tilst, herself, saying, "My name is Sharen Tilst and I'm VP of Sales at GNS. Three months after installing CloseProspects we reported a 12% profit increase and our customer satisfaction ratios jumped 47%." Remember a customer story is good; a customer testimonial is even more powerful.

Your Speeches
Step 1: Diagnose the PAIN

Find the most common PAIN of the attendees in the audience. Stay away from generalities and be as specific as possible about the PAIN. Select the most acute PAIN. Ask your audience if they agree with your diagnostic and identify a few head movements as a yes.

Step 2: Differentiate your CLAIMS

Choose your CLAIMS that correlate with the PAIN you have identified.

Step 3: Demonstrate the GAIN

Choose the proofs that are the most relevant to your audience as a group and that are the strongest.

Step 4: Deliver to the OLD BRAIN

Use all the Message Building Blocks described in this book: Grabber, Big Picture, CLAIMS, Proofs of GAIN, Handling Objections, and Closing.

You may insert your credentials into your speech, but preferably, do it after your Grabber. Your introduction should establish your credibility so the audience is open to receiving your information as an expert in your field. Make it short, but informative, precise, visual, and personal. Tell them why it's relevant for them to pay attention to you.

In his book *Leading Out Loud*, author Terry Pearce gives a great example of the best way to deliver credentials. Terry tells of the case of a young professional who was introduced to a business audience simply as an "environmental consultant" who would speak on the topic of "urban conservation". The consultant was prepared to supplement whatever introduction he received and proceeded to elaborate for the audience.

"I have been extremely fortunate to have spent most of my life educating myself for my work," he said. "I have spent almost 25 years in schools and over 30 years in the outdoors. I've traveled from the Arctic Ocean to the equator, climbed some of the highest peaks in Europe, and trekked through the jungles of Borneo. As an environmental consultant for six years, I've visited more garbage dumps than I care to remember. I've been involved with oil spills off the coast of Alaska and train wrecks in densely populated urban areas. My conclusion from all these experiences? We are not living a sustainable existence."

Go for impact. Remember, the way you deliver is key to getting and holding attention, and making the sale.

Keep the room cold and well-lighted. This will prevent your audience's OLD BRAINS from idling too quickly. Use real pictures, video clips and/or audiotapes. Involve the audience. Minimize the amount of text. Use key words, but 'tell' the content using all the techniques that make great selling events. Use variety in color, in voice, and in movements. If other presenters use PowerPoint, try using a flip chart if the room is not too big. Make it an absolute "must" to use at least one prop and several stories. Address the audience directly and individually.

Move from behind the podium. Use as much space as possible. Establish and maintain eye-contact with the people in the front rows. You should look, feel, and sound different from the other speakers--yet you should look, feel and sound similar and friendly to your audience.

Rehearse, rehearse, and rehearse. You don't have to learn your text word for word, but you should be able to make your presentation without reading. DO NOT READ your text at all costs and do not repeat what is already written on your slides. Your slides should support your presentation, not replace it. Remember, the OLD BRAIN is much more sensitive to your energy than to a spreadsheet, regardless of how good the numbers look.

Your Presentations

In today's world, it almost always requires three to four people to say "yes" before you get the order or commitment. If you are doing your job efficiently as a salesperson you need to meet all four deci-sion-influencers. Giving a formal presentation of your product is a very effective way of reaching the whole group at once.

We each have the same 24 hours in a day. The biggest differ-ence between those who are successful and those who are not is the way they make use of their time. I suggest that you focus your energy on your top accounts.

Invest a lot of time preparing. It's better to deliver one presen-tation a week and close at 30% than to do two presentations a week and close only 10%. For big-ticket items, there are few "one-call closes." The objective of your presentations should be to close, or to get a commitment to move the sales process forward.

If your diagnostic is correct, and the prospect acknowledges it, if you present your unique CLAIMS and back them up with solid Proofs of GAIN, and then you demonstrate beyond any doubt that you are the ONLY solution that can solve their PAIN, why would they further delay a decision? Every passing day would cause them to lose money. Bring this to the attention of their OLD BRAIN which should be highly sensitive to that fact!

Step 1: Diagnose the PAIN

Find as much as you can about the PAIN of your target group. No two prospects have exactly the same PAIN. The more specific you can be about their own PAIN, the faster you will reach their OLD BRAIN.

Ideally, you should have each prospect acknowledge your diag-nostic of their PAIN before the presentation. This way you will know for sure that what you are selling is a cure to their PAIN.

Go to your prospect's web site, read their newsletters, talk to people internally, find a pretext to set up a short one-on-one meet-ing prior to the big presentation to learn about or confirm their PAIN. Tell them, for example, that you are preparing for the presentation you have set-up in two weeks and you would like to confirm the PAIN you are assuming they have so that this presentation really zeros in on their most important issues and is a good investment of their time. It is smart to get early "buy-in" from each person before a general meeting.

In fact, you should invest most of your energy setting up these one-on-one meetings prior to D-day so that on D-day your sales presentation is 100% selling and 0% telling. D-day should be reserved to proving the value of your CLAIMS to solve their top PAIN.

The biggest issue is making sure you are going after the right PAIN. One of the most common mistakes is to prepare a presentation which attempts to solve a PAIN that the prospect doesn't even have. The key to successful formal presentations is to make sure your prospect acknowledges the PAIN that you have diagnosed prior to the meeting.

Step 2: Differentiate your CLAIMS

Learn as much as you can about your competitors. Choose your CLAIMS depending on the prospect's top PAIN and the competition you are facing. Once you have a thorough knowledge of your market, you can actually choose your CLAIMS from a library of possible options and just do a copy and paste. When you prepare your presentation, choose only the Message Building Blocks that you may have prepared for a prospect with the exact same PAIN and with the same competitive landscape.

If the PAIN and competitive situation between a previous prospect and this new one are different, you must redefine your CLAIMS. Remember, you must find or create something unique about your offering so you don't have to discount your price in order to be the most appealing. If you end up playing the pricing game with your prospect, it is because your skipped a step in the selling process and did not Demonstrate enough GAIN.

Step 3: Demonstrate the GAIN

Use only your strongest Proofs of GAIN. Choose the proofs that are the most relevant to that particular prospect.

Step 4: Deliver Impact to the OLD BRAIN

Besides your Proofs of GAIN, you should use a *Grabber* (to create a strong first impression), a Big Picture (to create understanding), and establish powerful CLAIMS (to help the prospect remember your unique benefits).

Prepare to customize everything about your message around their specific PAIN. Sometimes a small amount of customization like copying and pasting their logo somewhere in your presentation can go a long way in giving them the feeling you really are the only one who could cure their PAIN and your actions are totally dedicated to their benefit.

Customize Your Message

If your corporate sales process provides you with canned sales presentations, take the time to revise them based on the Four Steps to maximize your selling effectiveness. Carefully construct your message for maximum impact to the OLD BRAIN by using the Message Building Blocks. Do not underestimate the power of a Grabber, good stories, and strong *visuals*. Reorganize your Value Proposition with Proofs of GAIN so prospects can see the value without effort. Don't rely on your prospects to do the work: if *you* don't do the math of adding up the proven values of your three CLAIMS and subtracting your cost matrix, don't expect your prospects to.

Make it Short

Avoid any presentation that lasts longer than one hour. These types of events become 'telling' events, not 'selling' events.

Focus on Your Close

Repeat your CLAIMS one more time. Get some Positive Public Feedback by asking: "What do you think?" Listen openly to their feedback; answer any objections they may have. Then let them commit to the next step: "What is the next step?" If you thoroughly performed the four steps to increase your Selling, the only outcome that makes sense for them is to buy from you.

Your Job Interviews
Step 1: Diagnose the PAIN

Find as much as you can about the job you are applying for. Why are they recruiting? What PAIN are they experiencing now without somebody in this position? For executive positions, help the company refine their diagnostic: they might think they need somebody with a certain skill set, when in fact you can prove that they need something entirely different, maybe they need somebody with YOUR skill set.

Step 2: Differentiate your CLAIMS

Get a sense about the other candidates. Choose your CLAIMS accordingly. Listen to what skills they are looking for and listen carefully to what they say about you.

Step 3: Demonstrate the GAIN

Prepare your Proofs of GAIN: includes specific statistics and concrete evidence of your past achievements. For example, "In 5 years at ABC, under my management, sales grew 45%." Can you find a simple document that proves it?

In interviews, prepare to show your Proofs of GAIN. On a resume, include a testimonial by someone saying something relevant about you. You can use:

- a reference list with well recognizable names or companies
- quotes of customers or past employers
- recommendation letters, thank you notes, appreciation letters

Step 4: Deliver to the OLD BRAIN

Show the recruiter you are an expert at what you do. Demonstrate you are a perfect match for what they need. Be sure to deliver your message using the six stimuli: *self-centered, tangible, contrast, visual, emotion* and *beginning and end*.

Summarize the three main skills needed in the position. Craft your CLAIMS around these most-needed skills. Demonstrate you are unique. Use a prop, a story or a mini-drama as appropriate.

In an interview, make strong eye contact, and give a firm handshake. Use wording with "You". Don't talk about you; tell them what you could do for them.

In your resume, change the order of things. For example, if you can get a quote from one of your previous managers, insert it at the beginning after your objectives.

Show your passion for the job and the industry. Make sure you have other job options so your fearlessness is real: nobody wants to hire a desperate candidate. Reread the story about Agnes in the mini-drama section about Grabbers.

BRAINPOWER

- Increase your Selling Probability by Triggering the Only 6 Stimuli that Reach the True Decision Maker

- Assess Whether the PAIN is Financial, Strategic or Personal

- Focus on the Most Time Sensitive PAIN Areas

- Ensure that your Prospect Acknowledges his or her PAIN

- Start your Sales Process with Open Questions

- Use Diagnostic Dialogue as a Shortcut to Assess the Main PAIN of your Prospect

- Selling Without a Thorough Diagnostic is Like Providing a Cure When You're Not Sure What the Disease Is

- Always Sell Something that is Perceived to be Totally Unique

- Claim that You are the Only One Who Does or Has Something Specific

- Treat your Solution as an Invention and Build your Message Firmly on your CLAIMS

- Don't just Talk about your GAIN, Prove it!

- Make the GAIN the Center of your Message

- Make a Strong First Impression by Creating a Powerful Grabber

- Create a Big Picture, a Simple, Visual Representation of how your Product can Positively Impact the World of your Prospect

- Make your CLAIMS Memorable by Repeating them

- To Make Them Memorable, Wordsmith Your CLAIMS to Be the Shortest and Simplest Possible

- Present Concrete Evidence to Gain Your Prospect's Confidence

- Reframe the Objection by Presenting a Positive Side to it

- Repeat your CLAIMS and Then Get "Positive Public Feedback" to Close Messages Instantly Become Old-Brain-Friendly when Using 'You'

- Measure your "Credibility Factor" in Order to Increase Your Selling Effectiveness

- Be Fearless and Maintain Low Attachment to the Outcome

- To Be Trusted: Look, Feel and Sound like your Prospect's Best Friend

- It's not What you Say; it's How you Say it That Matters Most

- Varying your Voice Reflects Good Energy and Projects Feeling

- To Build Trust, Make Eye Contact for At Least 5 Seconds

- A Sharp Contrast Helps Your Prospect's OLD BRAIN Make a Decision More Quickly and Easily

- No Emotion, No Decision. Powerful Emotions Mark Your OLD BRAIN and Reach Straight to Its Core

- Most Messages are Auditory by Default: make them more Visual and Kinesthetic

- The OLD BRAIN Cannot Tell the Difference Between Reality and a Well-Told Story

- Less is More

RESOURCES

Title	Author	Topic
The Evolution of Consciousness	Robert Ornstein	Brain Research
How the Brain Works	Leslie Hart	Brain Research
Fear Itself	Rush Dozier	Brain Research
The Emotional Brain	Joseph LeDoux	Brain Research
Descartes Error	Antonio Damasio	Neurosciences
Emotional Intelligence	Daniel Goleman	Brain and Intelligence
The Primal Teen	Barbara Strauch	Neuroscience, Behavior
Executive EQ	R. Cooper, A. Sawaf	Leadership
Synchronicity	Joseph Jaworski	Leadership
Leadership in Paradoxical Age	Noel Tichy	Leadership
The Leadership Challenge	James Kouzes	Leadership
Influencing with Integrity	Genie Laborde	NLP
The Magic of Rapport	Jerry Richardson	NLP
The 22 Immutable Laws of Marketing	Al Ries, Jack Trout	Marketing
Strategy Pure and Simple	Michel Robert	Marketing, Strategy
Crossing the Chasm	Geoffrey Moore	Marketing, Strategy
Unleashing the Killer App	Larry Downes	Marketing
How Customers Think	Gerald Zaltman	Marketing
The Clue Train Manifesto	Locke, Levine, 1 Weinberger	E-commerce and voice

Title	Author	Topic
You've got to be Believed to be Heard	Bert Decker	Presentation Skills Brain Research
Integrity Selling	Ron Willingham	Sales
Strategic Selling	Miller and Heiman	Sales
Samurai Selling	C. Laughlin, K. Sage	Sales
Presenting to Win	Jerry Weisman	Presentation Skills
Presentation Plus	David People	Sales, Presentations
Presentation	Daria Price Bowman	Presentation Skills
Delivering Dynamic Presentations	Ralph Hillman	Presentation Skills
Leading out Loud	Terry Pearce	Public Speaking
Loud and Clear: How to Prepare and Deliver Effective Business and Technical Presentations.	George Morrisey and Thomas Sechrest	Public Speaking, Presentation
The Prospect is King	Lee Harris	Prospect Service, Sales
The 7 Habits of Highly Effective People	Steven Covey	Business Efficiency
In Search of Excellence	Tom Peters	Business
The One-Minute Manager	Ken Blanchard	Business, Management
On Dialogue	David Bohm	Communication Theory

TRADEMARKS AND COPYRIGHTS

All logos, trademarks and copyrights belong to the their respective companies and are reprinted with express permission.

Company	Product	Point Illustrated
Air Canada	Air travel	Big Picture
BMW	Car	Auditory
CareerBuilder	Headhunter	Big Picture
CarsDirect.com	Car shopping online	CLAIMS
DrugFreeAmerica.com	Parental awareness	Emotion
InFocus	Projector	Claim
IBM	E-Business Consulting	GAIN
Linux	Open Source model	Visual
Microsoft	Visio	Big Picture
NationWide	Insurance	CLAIMS
Office Depot	Office Supplies	Grabber
Smirnoff	Vodka	Grabber
Sprint PCS	Cellular phone	CLAIMS